Sport: A Very Short Introduction

VERY SHORT INTRODUCTIONS are for anyone wanting a stimulating and accessible way in to a new subject. They are written by experts, and have been translated into more than 40 different languages.

The Series began in 1995, and now covers a wide variety of topics in every discipline. The VSI library now contains over 350 volumes—a Very Short Introduction to everything from Psychology and Philosophy of Science to American History and Relativity—and continues to grow in every subject area.

Very Short Introductions available now:

Available soon:

For more information visit our website

www.oup.co.uk/general/vsi/

Mike Cronin

SPORT

A Very Short Introduction

OXFORD
UNIVERSITY PRESS

OXFORD
UNIVERSITY PRESS

Great Clarendon Street, Oxford, OX2 6DP,
United Kingdom

Oxford University Press is a department of the University of Oxford.
It furthers the University's objective of excellence in research, scholarship,
and education by publishing worldwide. Oxford is a registered trade mark of
Oxford University Press in the UK and in certain other countries

Published in the United States of America by Oxford University Press
198 Madison Avenue, New York, NY 10016, United States of America

British Library Cataloguing in Publication Data

Data available

Library of Congress Control Number: 2014943271

ISBN 978-0-19-968834-0

Printed in Great Britain by
Ashford Colour Press Ltd, Gosport, Hampshire

For Moynagh

Contents

Acknowledgements

This book would not have been possible without the opportunities granted to me over the years to teach and research in the area of sport. In this I thank my colleagues at the International Centre for Sports History and Culture at De Montfort University, and those at Boston College. At Boston College Ireland my ever present friends and colleagues always provide a wonderful working environment, and have always given much inspiration and support. I would particularly like to acknowledge the stimulation given to me over the years by the work and support of four sports scholars, namely Doug Booth, Jeff Hill, Dan Nathan, and Murray Phillips, who have pushed a cultural awareness of sport that is helping redefine the field. A small group of people provided day to day motivation and advice, and some also read drafts of the book. In all that they did, these people helped me focus, spotted the gaps, and shaped the work, and so a huge debt of gratitude to Robert Colls, Mark Duncan, Kevin Kenny, Tara Magdalinski, Dilwyn Porter, and Paul Rouse. Most central in all my engagements with sport, in life and in the classroom, and through the writing of this book, has been the friendship and advice of Richard Holt. Few people know as much as him about the history of sport, and his eye for detail and style make him a wonderful reader to have on board.

The staff at Oxford University Press were a delight to work with, and Jenny Nugee, Emma Ma, and Carrie Hickman all helped guide me through a quite daunting process and made it an altogether pleasant process.

All the various members of my family were, as always, quite wonderful, but particular thanks and a huge debt of appreciation to the three people that share my life each day, for their unquestioning love, support, and direction, namely Moynagh, Ellen, and Samson.

List of illustrations

Introduction

> Sport creates a bond between contemporaries that lasts a
> lifetime. It also gives your life structure, discipline and a
> genuine, sincere, pure fulfilment that few other areas of
> endeavour provide.
>
> Bob Cousey, Boston Celtics Basketball player of the 1950s.

What is 'sport' and why has the urge to run or jump, to wrestle or
master a moving ball individually, or in a team, been part of
human culture for so long? Is sport a source of virtue or, as George
Orwell put it, 'war minus the shooting'? Sport harnesses the
human instinct for play and the joy of movement in the cause of
competition. Who is the strongest, the fastest, and the most
skilful? Male prowess was at the heart of sport before the Ancient
Greeks established the Olympic Games. But is our enjoyment of
playing ourselves the same as the pleasure of watching others
compete? Is the appeal of spectator sport primarily aesthetic or is
it dramatic? Or is it the sense of collective identity and sociability
which draws us in; being part of the crowd, especially being a 'fan',
supporting the same team, temporarily escaping into another
world of simpler allegiances and enthusiasm?

Over the decades sport has been described in many different ways.
When a finely tuned gymnast completes the perfect floor routine
or a soccer player elegantly executes a pass, observers will speak of

sporting bodies and their practices as beautiful and artistic. In the 1970s and 1980s when European soccer supporters were engaged in acts of hooliganism on terraces across the continent, sport seemingly provided the evidence that the game's core following of urban, white working class men were locked into a downward spiral of degenerate violence. The Soviet writer Maxim Gorky held the view that 'bourgeois sport has a single clear cut purpose, to make men even more stupid than they are'. The film, *Raging Bull* (1980), starring Robert de Niro as the late 1940s American boxer, Jake La Motta, is regularly listed as one of the best films ever made, and stands alongside *Million Dollar Baby* (2004), *Rocky* (1976), and *The Fighter* (2010) as a genre of sporting films that have succeeded as major critical and box office films for their cultural depictions of the incongruous mix of violence and honour that lies at the heart of boxing.

Sport has a socio-cultural presence resulting from its daily performance on the pitch, the television screen, in print, and online, and has also been reimagined in literary form with works such as Bernard Malamud's *The Natural* (1952), David Storey's *This Sporting Life* (1960), Richard Ford's *The Sportswriter* (1986), or Chad Harbach's *The Art of Fielding* (2011) capturing the narrative beauty and complexities of male relationships with different sports. Visual artists, from ancient Greek sculptors, through to Henry Raeburn's painting *The Reverend Robert Walker Skating on Duddingston Lock* (1795), George Bellows depiction of a prize fight, *Stag at Sharkey's* (1909), or Umberto Boccioni's futurist *Dynamism of a Cyclist* (1913) all represented the movement and physicality that is central to all sport. And then there are always the boys who follow their sporting heroes and dream of being the next David Beckham (soccer), Le Bron James (basketball), or Sachin Tendulkar (cricket).

In each of these multiple ways in which sport has been portrayed and the meanings that have been applied to it, there remains for the most part one constant common factor. Each has conventionally described men's sports, and this association between various masculinities and sport is so naturalized that media coverage has to distinguish women's sports as a separate category. Outside scholarly research, the assumed synergy between masculinity and sport goes unremarked. At the very heart of contemporary sport, and in its history, there exists a gender blindness. Sport emerged to entertain, train, and build men's bodies: to instil in them a moral, ethical, and physical code that would ensure their passage through life and maintain the masculine hegemony that existed in wider society. Such male sporting bodies were part and parcel of the nation building process, and were later transformed by the media, in all its guises, into a form of commoditized entertainment where the exploits of the male athlete dominate the daily coverage of sport.

In the modern era one thing is clear: elite male sport is big business and a huge box office attraction. It is estimated that 900 million people across the globe watched the opening ceremony of the London 2012 Olympics, 612 million tuned in for the 2010 soccer World Cup final, and that some 300 million watched the 2012 finals of both the US Superbowl and the European Champions League final. Given that increasing numbers of people engage with these major sporting events not through their television but online, the reach of such spectacles increases further. The economics associated with the popularity of men's sport is reflected in its selling power. A 30-second advertisement slot on US television during Superbowl 2013 cost $4 million. In the same year, the UK rights to show the European Champions League for three years were sold for £897 million, and the ten-year regional rights for Indian Premier League cricket sold for $1.3 billion. The elite players certainly benefit from the huge incomes that sport generates, and in 2012 the estimated incomes from prize money, salaries, and sponsorship for the three highest paid sportsmen in the world ranged from Kobe Bryant (basketball) $62 million, Roger Federer (tennis) $72 million, and Tiger Woods (golf) $78 million. In contrast, the top three earning women athletes, all tennis players, were Maria Sharapova, Li Na, and Serena Williams whose earnings totalled $27 million, $18 million, and $16 million respectively. Sharapova's income would have earned her only 29th place in the list of high earning males.

Sport, no matter how transitory the experience (the length of a match or tournament), is a constant at the heart of contemporary daily life. The way that sport has been understood, its values and ideologies, its very use in society has been transformed across history. In language the meaning of the word has similarly changed. In the 15th century sport denoted an activity providing diversion, entertainment, or fun. By the 18th and 19th century sport meant hunting, shooting, and fishing. After the industrial revolutions around the world, it referred to activities of physical exertion and skill that were regulated by set rules and regulations.

Nowadays, while still a mass participation activity enjoyed by millions, in its various forms, the overriding perception and imagery of the sporting world is that which is enacted in an ever running series of seasons, tournaments, World Cups, and Olympic games. Sport in its cultural and media forms is currently a predominantly male world of million-dollar salaries and endorsement packages, blanket multi-platform media coverage, and endless cliché. It is also a business that struggles to balance its constant retelling and re-presentation of its core historical and philosophical messages, the spirit of fair play and the heroism of athletic endeavour, with an underbelly of violence, cheating, and corruption which regularly comes to the fore.

Chapter 1
Origins

The first sports and games were played in various parts of the world, in a variety of different forms. They appear recognizable to us as sports or forms of play, but they are radically different to what we now understand as modern sport. Over the centuries sport has progressed from what has been described as a physical form of ritual, to the modern sporting era where the tightly ruled contests rely on records and measurement in the form of scores, distances, and times. What is understood of ancient sport has largely been recovered through archaeology (texts and material culture), and the specific meanings and practices associated with such partially recovered games often remains unclear.

Early play

On the evidence found on carved stone slabs and a bronze figurine discovered in Iraq, it appears that the Sumerians were some of the first humans to record their sporting activity, as wrestlers, around 3000 BC. Later, the ancient Egyptians featured an elite that practised a wide range of sports and, in light of their burial practices and the material remains of their civilization, much of this has been reconstructed. The elite demonstrated their strength in boxing, swimming, running, hunting, archery, and different forms of equestrian sports.

Reliefs in Egyptian tombs and pyramids depict an array of sporting exploits that stress the physical strength of the pharaoh, which in turn underscored his ability to rule. In one temple frieze Egyptian soldiers are shown wrestling Nubians, a people from modern Sudan, who had long practised the sport and this demonstrates not only the power and reach of Egyptian rule, but also the wide dispersal of early sporting practices. The contest depicted on the frieze takes place in front of the pharaoh and a small crowd, which would have comprised members of the upper echelons of society. The role of the pharaoh, in both life and death, is vital to understanding the function of ancient Egyptian sport. Many of the Egyptian sporting activities, and those across the ancient world, would have taken the form of funeral games or annual contests to remember those who had passed on. The dead pharaohs functioned as mediators between the gods and man. As such the annual veneration and remembrance of them through worship and sport was a key factor in maintaining order. In this context, sport, while possibly functioning as a form of entertainment or preparation for combat, was first and foremost driven by the demands of a ritual which honoured the preceding generations.

In other parts of the ancient world a range of different sports and games were pursued, and like the Egyptians the impulse behind their practice gives the impression that they were ritualistic and religious. In North America, the native game was a stick and ball game that preceded modern lacrosse. In Ireland, written records suggest hurling, another stick and ball game, was played from 1200 BC, and that practising the game was a key component in the male journey to adulthood that prepared them to be warriors.

In China, Confucian teachings, and those of Buddhism later, led to an ambivalent attitude towards physically violent and combat sports. Often the search for spiritual harmony won out over the quest for sporting excitement. Exercises such as tai chi were popular, but so was archery as a ceremonial practice that was approved of by Confucians. The dominant early game in China, despite its occasional physicality, was cuju. The game was referred to in Sima Qian's epic history of the country, *Shiji*, written around 90 BC. Cuju involved trying to kick a ball through a net, and it has been claimed that the game was invented by the Yellow Emperor around 2500 BC to train men for the military. The game became highly popular in China, and spread from the military, into the royal court and the elite of society. By the time of the Song dynasty, 960–1279, cuju had become popular through all levels of society, including women, and the royal court even maintained a team of professional cuju players.

Japan was the home, from the 8th century AD of Sumo, a highly ritualized form of wrestling (Figure 1). It held a position at the heart of the imperial court calendar, and was a practice that spread widely across the country. The warrior class, with war always in mind, were expert archers, and records remain detailing regular competitions amongst nobles and members of the imperial family. In ancient Persia a game akin to polo was popular, and again the impulse behind this seems to have been to hone horsemanship skills in preparedness for war. In India yoga, in various forms, was important, as were other practices which spoke to religious beliefs (whether Hindu, Buddhist, or Muslim) such as wrestling, grappling, and polo.

In South and Central America, from around 1200 BC, the Mesoamerican ball game held sway. The game was played with a rubberized ball, and took place in stone-built ball courts, the remains of which were uncovered by 19th century European archaeologists. The Mesoamerican ball game had significant cultural and political importance. The games were seen as a way in which neighbouring kingdoms could compete with each other and settle disputes without reverting to warfare. The contests also had important religious symbolism with the game said to mirror the ball court of the heavens and the perpetual battle between day and night. The Mesoamerican game additionally served as a fertility rite relating to both human and botanical renewal.

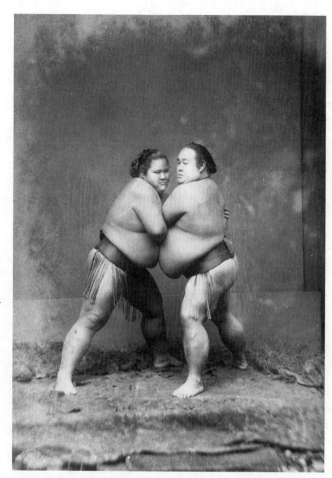

1. The ancient sports of Japan offer a counterpoint to the western narrative of the development of sport. Sumo wrestling has ancient roots, and became a popular spectator sport from the 1600s. Here two Sumo wrestlers (*c.*1890) are shown in their traditional mawashi belts

Ancient Greece

In these earliest games the specific localized sporting practice was closely tied with the elites of society, and had significant ritual elements. Sport was further developed by the ancient Greeks and Romans who made it a visible component of the social life of their states and societies. From about 1600 BC, and the growth of Greek power and stability, sporting festivals became a regular occurrence and were often associated with the funerals of royalty. Such games were said to give pleasure to the wandering soul of the honoured person, and were steeped in religious mythology. These contests, as recorded by Greek writers such as Pausanius and Homer, served to reinforce the value of life in the face of death, while honouring those who had died. The relationship between the Greeks and their gods was a close one, and nothing, including sport, failed to be influenced by the actions of those gods. Even sportsmen knew that their success or failure, in a contest, was a decision made by the gods. In the early Greek funeral games the ranks of the competitors were comprised of the wealthy and powerful. While chariot racing was the most prestigious sport, there was also boxing and wrestling, foot races, duels, discus, archery, and javelin. The competitions were for individuals and not teams, were fiercely contested, and the winner received a prize that was usually offered by a wealthy patron. As the athletes competed for prizes, the word athlete emerged from the Greek, meaning someone who competes for a reward. The spectators at the funeral games were all male, all members of the military, and laid wagers with each other on the outcome of the various events.

With Greek power and prestige stretching over centuries, so games and sports became more organized, more frequent, and participation extended beyond a small elite. Funeral games, which had largely been the preserve of the military, developed into athletic festivals. These events, which may have taken place over the course of one day, and at larger festivals over several, were a mixture of sporting contest and religious festival. By 500 BC four festivals dominated, namely the Pythian Games at Delphi, the Isthmian Games at Corinth, the Nemean Games at Nemean, and the most famous of all, the Olympic Games, held every four years for prizes of an olive wreath in honour of Zeus, at Olympia. Olympia had emerged as a significant site around 1000 BC when it became a shrine to Zeus.

The Games at Olympia began later, in 776 BC, and functioned as a religious, sporting, and cultural event. To compete at Olympia an athlete had to be a free-born Greek male, and would take part as the representative of the various city states that attended the Games. City states actively used the Games, and any success achieved by their athletes, to elevate their prestige and demonstrate their prominence within the Greek world. During the period of the Games an Olympic truce was enforced so that the event could pass off without disruption. All athletes competing at the Games did so in honour of Zeus, and had to pledge, in his name, to compete fairly and to respect all rules. Any athlete who transgressed the rules was fined by the organizers. The first Games featured a lone foot race, but with the passing years more foot races, and then other sports were added. The list of featured sports would eventually grow to include foot races, boxing, wrestling, chariot racing, the pentathlon, and a series of throwing events.

For the first two centuries of the Games at Olympia there were no permanent buildings to speak of. From around 550 BC building began, and the site grew to include a temple, treasure houses, a council house, and, specifically for the sports themselves, a hippodrome and stadium. Alongside the stadium was built a gymnasium and palaestrae (wrestling schools). It is estimated that the stadium could house 40,000 spectators. Such a large stadium demonstrates how important the games were to Greek society. At its peak, the Games were spread over five days (two and a half days dedicated to the sporting events, the remainder to celebrate the gods), and the winners of each event were awarded an olive branch and other prizes. Winning athletes were revered in their home cities, and were often further rewarded by the authorities on their return home.

While those competing in events such as the chariot races, which required financial outlay in terms of equipment and horses, were a self-financing elite, lower class athletes in the athletic contests relied on patronage. As the athletes competed for the glory of the city state, they were supported by leading citizens, and from taxes paid to the public funds. This would ensure that they were housed and fed, and their training and travel costs covered. Such athletes would not simply have competed at Olympia, but would have travelled around Greece and beyond, attending all the main competitions. It is a fantasy to imagine that all Greek athletes competed solely for the honour of their city and the gods. Many of them were effectively full-time athletes and given that they earned their material comforts from competition, they were effectively professionals. The glory of these athletes was further celebrated and the feats of the winners praised by poets in attendance at games such as those at Olympia, who would recite verses and sing odes praising them. No women were allowed to compete at the games, and apart from the priestess, Demeter, they were also excluded from the event as spectators.

Ancient Rome

The Roman Empire's military was one of the key forces that lay behind its success. The militarism of Rome meant that the Romans initially favoured physical exercises over play for its own sake. While the Roman Emperors and other wealthy citizens acted as patrons of Greek sports, they did not survive at the centre of Roman life. In 186 BC Greek athletes were brought to Rome to demonstrate their skills, but they received a mixed reception. Across the centuries, Emperors such as Nero, Tiberius, Julius Caesar, and Pompey all staged major Greek athletic events either in Rome or in Greece, and Hadrian in 131 AD staged a major new games in Athens and had the stadium there rebuilt. Despite the personal enthusiasm of some of Rome's rulers, and the political and diplomatic value in supporting Greek sport, the Romans remained suspicious. They were unimpressed that Greek athletes chose to compete naked, and many held that the Greek gymnasium was a place of vice and homosexuality.

The Romans preferred sports that were for a purpose, those games that prepared men for the military and made them warriors. As such sports such as wrestling, boxing, and javelin throwing were preferred over those Greek sports, such as foot races, which had minimal military value. However, it was the spectacle of chariot racing and gladiatorial combat that was most popular in Rome and which holds sway in the cultural representation of the Roman Empire as with the films *Spartacus* (1960) and *Gladiator* (2000) and the television series *Spartacus: Blood and Sand* (2010–13). In stadia such as Rome's Colosseum, which was capable of holding up to 80,000 spectators, gladiators would battle each other or wild animals. The contests were brutal, but hugely popular. The Roman calendar was full of holidays in honour of various deities. These days became the focus for Roman sporting competition which worked as spectacles to be consumed by spectators. Such events, organized by Rome's political leaders, kept the populace entertained, and the practice was satirized by the Roman poet Juvenal, who argued that rather than caring about civic duties and responsibilities the populace were passive and anxiously hoped 'for just two things: bread and circuses'.

Chariot races were contests between charioteers, usually slaves, who steered two-wheeled chariots seven times around an oval track. Betting by the crowd was a feature of the day, and the chariots owned by wealthy Romans who competed with each other, in the way of modern horse race owners, for a succession of prizes and purses. Equally popular with the Roman crowds were the gladiatorial contests. The day's schedule of events began with animal fights. Sometimes these fights were between different types of animals (in Nero's time 400 tigers were brought to the

Colosseum to fight bulls and elephants), or else contests that pitched condemned criminals against the animals. The gladiatorial battles occupied the afternoon schedule, and the fighters drawn from the ranks of criminals, slaves, and prisoners from foreign wars. They were trained hard and had to fight, if they survived each contest, for three years to achieve their freedom. The large crowds who gathered to watch the slaughter bet heavily on the outcome, and delighted in the opportunity, when a gladiator was near fatally wounded, to give the thumbs up or down for mercy or death. Such was the popularity of the gladiatorial battle that smaller versions of the Colosseum had been built throughout Italy and the Roman Empire by the end of the second century.

The Roman sports were bloodthirsty, and functioned to entertain a populace. These were not games to take part in, but rather to watch. Only the condemned and the enslaved fought to the death. With the appearance of Christianity in the Roman world, criticisms of such an inhuman and pagan spectacle emerged. The eventual emergence of Christianity as the dominant religion in Rome led to a change in the sporting landscape. By the 4th century condemned prisoners were no longer forced to take part in gladiatorial contests, the names of pagan gods were removed from the list of holidays thereby reducing the number of days on which gladiatorial contests could take place, and chariot racing was forbidden on Sundays. The conversion to Christianity of the Emperor Constantine brought an end to the brutality and idolatry of the gladiatorial spectacle, which was finally deemed unpalatable. Around 404 the sport was officially abolished. The reforming zeal of the Christians turned on all events that were staged in honour of pre-Christian gods, and across the Mediterranean world a series of sporting events and festivals that had been staged for centuries in honour of Greek or pagan gods and deities were banned. As the Roman Empire first retreated to the East, and then collapsed completely, its organized sporting spectacles, without strong patronage and opposed by Christians, disappeared from the calendar.

After the fall of the Roman Empire and the relative lack of political and military stability or wealth across many parts of Europe sport became far less organized than it had been under the Greeks or the Romans. Rather than a sporting landscape that was ordered, where the elite acted as patrons and planners, and where a worshipful element had been at the core of the event, sports through the Middle Ages were more impromptu and more likely to be organized by or for the lower classes of society. There did remain an important residue of elite organization and participation in certain sports during the period, and the Catholic Church would emerge as an agency that would seek to control the playing of various games.

The Middle Ages

The impetus for the staging of sporting contests in the Middle Ages was informed by the calendar, and it was a series of Christian holy days that became the occasions on which sport was most regularly played. These sports were different from the spectacles of Olympic Games and gladiatorial contest that dominated in Greece and Rome. They were participatory and localized and not organized by the state. Across Europe there were many regional variations for the games that were played, but at holiday times such as Christmas, Shrove Tuesday, or Easter, acts of observance were followed by a festival or fair where games and competitions took place. Many of these were quite rudimentary and included running or sack races, competitions of strength, and feats of endurance.

For the elites of the Middle Ages the now well-established pattern of combining military skills with sport, as many of the ancient civilizations had done, continued in the context of advancing military technologies. Archery was a favoured sport, as were other events that displayed strength and skill such as jousting, and those related to various forms of hunting. In the age of the chivalrous knight, war games, known as tournaments, became the venue for aristocrats to engage in mock combat. Kingdoms and clans competed against each other, personified in the form of their champion, in front of crowds, from all classes, gathered to witness the spectacle.

The high point of the tournament across Europe was the period from the 12th to the 14th century and at times the associated carnage of such events evoked the Roman gladiatorial contests. Despite the violence that often accompanied the tournament, the intended spirit of the events was supposed to be altogether different. Knights, although effectively existing to defend their homeland in times of war, also lived by a code of chivalry, bound by their honour to serve God and their king. In many ways the chivalrous concept that lay behind the conduct of the knight was transferred in part to their sporting contests, and codes of behaviour, especially in how they conducted themselves in competition and the manner in which they treated their opponent, were expected to be observed. The knights were well rewarded for their exertions, and travelled widely to compete. The whole feeling of carnival around the tournaments was important, and the performance at the events was a central feature. Indeed these tournaments can best be understood to be as an acting out of courtly life through pageantry and spectacle. No peasants were allowed to compete in tournament events, although side shows featuring cudgelling and wrestling did afford them an opportunity to take part. In a similar vein there were also foot races that were open to lower class women who competed for prizes. Elite women did not involve themselves in the sports of the tournament but did join the crowds of spectators to watch.

Ball games

One of the key developments of this period was the rise of the ball game. The Moors, who invaded Europe in the 8th century, brought with them various ball and stick games, and these proved popular in those areas that they colonized, notably Spain and southern France. As such these ball games became part of the holiday calendar, and were played notably at Easter. In France there are many 9th and 10th century references to ball games being part of the rituals of the Easter celebration, and this tying together of worship, ritual, and sport was initially supported by the Church. The spread of Catholicism across Europe during this period was important as it heralded the observance of the Sabbath. With free time on their hands after church services, men across the continent began to play various forms of sport, most notably different forms of ball, and stick and ball, games. However, neither Church nor state would necessarily welcome the forms that these new games took on and the apparent dangers they posed.

One form of ball game which emerged in 16th century Florence was calcio. The game was played between Epiphany and Lent in the Piazza Santa Croce. It was a game reserved for the aristocratic young, who formed two teams of 27. There were referees, and the game lays claim to the first written sporting rules, which were published in 1580. The rules did not control how players could wrestle the ball from each other, and as a result calcio became known for its violence. In 1574, the visiting Henry III of France observed the game and noted that calcio was too small to be a real war but too cruel to be a game.

The unruliness of calcio was mirrored elsewhere in Europe, and particularly in Britain in another form of ball game, folk football. The game took place on holy days, particularly Shrove Tuesday, and involved a challenge between neighbouring villages. The team size was unlimited and the aim was to move a ball (which in fact could be an inflated bladder or a cask of ale) to a defined geographical point across the fields that linked the villages. Given the size of the teams, which could run into the hundreds, the accompanying drink that was taken, the lack of rules, and the presence of local rivalries, the games were highly charged and violent. Injuries were common and death not unknown. Such was the chaos around the game that between the 13th and mid-17th century there were more than 30 local and royal laws that banned or at least restricted the game. The popularity of the game meant that it moved into the cities at times, spaces that were completely unsuited to such a contest. As a result football was banned by the London authorities in the 14th century, and by those in Manchester in the 15th.

In fact the whole history of folk football is one of attempts to control the game. It was seen as unruly, boisterous, and violent, perceived not as the scene of gentlemen playing, but rather the site of ungodly chaos. The 14th century Church in England banned the game from being played on its property, and also forbade the clergy from taking part in the game. The story was the same in France where the Church moved against the game, and also found an ally in the monarchy, who found the sight of the mobs gathering to play fearful, a threat to the order of society, and potentially revolutionary. In England the royal reaction, while concerned that the games were a threat to the public peace, also worried that such ramshackle popular activities prevented men preparing properly for their service to the nation. In the 14th century various laws were enacted in England and Ireland that forbade the citizenry from playing football, instructing them instead to spend more time with their bows and arrows in readiness for war.

Ball games were also recorded elsewhere across the globe. The Inuit people of Greenland were observed playing a football game in 1586, and in colonial America the native American game of pahsaheman was noted in 1610. Early arrivals in Australia observed the foot and ball game Mam Grook being played by aboriginals, and in New Zealand the Maori people were witnessed playing Ki-o-rahi. That games featuring a ball being propelled by players proved so popular and emerged in various forms in unconnected places around the globe does speak to the human need to amuse and entertain themselves, and the link between man and ball is a long standing feature of human civilization. This has been referred to as the ludic theory of human nature and marks the enjoyment of play as something separate from the basic human function of survival. Such play, which is about fun, is also creative, imaginative, and representative.

A host of other sports emerged during the medieval period. One such game was stoolball, where a ball was propelled by one player to knock over an object, originally a milking stool, while another attempted to defend the target. Initially this was done with the hand, but later a stick or club was used. In the various forms of stoolball, the origins of modern cricket and baseball can be found. Bowls, whether bowling at a target or trying to knock down a cone (or skittle) was popular across Europe, particularly in England, France, Germany, and the Netherlands. In Scotland, the Low Countries and the Nordic countries, the cold winters allowed the spirit of bowling at a target to morph into curling and the sliding of stones across the ice. In response to the violence of the tournaments, the Church supported, indeed were the originators of, more sedate and less violent sports; what began as a form of handball in French monasteries spread beyond the walls of the religious enclaves and became royal tennis, a game much beloved by the monarchy of France and England. The evidence for the opulence and built structures necessary for the game can still be viewed at Hampton Court in London, which was built by Henry VIII in the 1520s so that he could play the game.

Following the rough and tumble of various football games, the later Renaissance period witnessed the transition of many of the aspects of the medieval tournament into sports that showcased skill. Sports that came to the fore were more concerned with bodily aesthetics than brute force. The horse events of the tournament became horse racing, and various courses sprung up around major towns. In Siena, Italy, the horse race took the form of the palio that pitted nobles from the different areas of the city against each other. In a similar vein, archery, the skill that had been seen as essential for men in preparation for war, had been made obsolete by military advances and became a sport practised purely for competition. Royal tennis continued to spread across Europe, and golf, a game first referenced in the 15th century, appeared in Scotland, England, and the Netherlands.

By the late Renaissance humanist thinkers began arguing that bodies should be trained physically to embrace the beauty of the classical model rather than taking part in sports based around military training or competition. In this space, gymnastics appeared as a way of training, strengthening, and beautifying the body, while in France and Italy from the 17th century fencing, as an art form and not a sport, flourished. Bodily poise and movement were valued in this period, and the elites mixed the grace of dancing with sport, and increasingly the sons of the elite were finding that some form of sporting or physical practice was becoming a feature of their education. It was an important step as the Renaissance awareness of the body would inform the later spread of gymnastics across Central Europe, but also led in time to the emergence of physical education as a discipline. Control was, by the close of the Renaissance, a central issue. Aesthetic sporting practices attempted to control the body and its movements, while the law was employed to prevent folk football and manage the use of public space, thereby limiting the opportunities for the lower classes to engage themselves in a violent and disorderly pastime. Control over how sports were actually played was also being developed, as happened with calcio, with the introduction of rules that regulated what took place on the field of play.

A wholesale attempt to recapture the supposed glories and sensibilities of the ancient Greek Olympics would wait until the late 19th century. By the late 16th century sport, in different forms, and centred on the interests of various classes, had emerged as an important feature of people's social life. From the ancient wrestlers of Sumeria, and on through the centuries, in a host of settings, sports and games had established themselves as activities that had captured the imagination and that people wanted to play and watch. However, in observing these origins of sport, caution is advised. These early sporting practices were forms of play, all of which are culturally and historically specific. Examples given here point to moments of genesis and change, but the wider history of non-western bodily practices also has to be acknowledged. The history of sport is not a simple progression from Ancient Greece to the stadia of contemporary sport, but rather a complex narrative of non-lineal changes that were constantly fractured by time and place.

Chapter 2
Modern

The development of modern sports, as we would recognize them now, was primarily a product of the second half of the 19th century. However, prior to the coalescence of various forces that would lead to the rise of sport in its modern, codified, and rational form, there were a series of key building blocks that would inform the Victorian development of sporting activity. The common practice of playing sport on feast days and Sundays had led to the popular spread of games such as folk football. The brief period of Puritan domination in 17th century Britain and colonial America had introduced a moral view of bodily activity into the frame and had argued against various immoral activities associated with sport, such as gambling. In a sporting sense this would be the puritanical legacy. The Puritans desire to control sport and to introduce a moral code into the way games were played would come to the fore again in the Victorian era.

In the 18th century enthusiasm for sport grew steadily in Britain, and especially among the elite of society. In the period after the English Civil War and the restoration of the monarchy in 1660, conditions for a growing interest in all forms of leisure, and in particular sport, were present in Britain in a manner in which they were absent elsewhere. The nation's power and influence across the globe was growing, as was its domestic wealth. While

Britain would fight wars during the 18th and 19th centuries these were always fought on foreign soil. Britain's domestic security was underpinned by its island status and the strength of its navy. Without the need, as elsewhere in Europe, for a large standing army, and during the long-running domestic peace following the restoration of the monarchy, British attentions turned to transforming the agricultural and industrial landscape which would eventually revolutionize the nation. At the heart of society, in the form of landowners, investors and businessmen was a group of socially elite men—the gentry—who were both wealthy and had abundant leisure time. In sport, these groups, led by the monarchy, had found a shared arena for their pursuit of leisure activity.

The advent of rules

One of the most significant sports participated in and enjoyed by the elite, and also watched by the masses, was horse racing. Charles II built himself a racecourse at Windsor, and patronized Newmarket, which grew as the town where the fashionable sent their horses to be reared and trained for racing. Charles began the Newmarket Town Plate race in 1664, and was so personally wrapped up in the sport that he wrote the rules himself. Later monarchs were also great supporters and patrons of racing, William III as a gambler, and Queen Anne as an owner, breeder, and founder, in 1711, of Ascot racecourse. The close ties between the monarchy and the sport were evident in the inaugural race at Ascot, for a purse of 100 guineas, which was given the title, Her Majesty's Plate. As someone involved in the breeding of horses, Queen Anne was closely tied to the importation of important sires into Britain. Of all modern thoroughbred racehorses, over 90 per cent are direct descendants of one of Queen Anne's imports, the Darley Arabian.

Clearly one of the great attractions of horse racing was the opportunity it afforded people to gamble. However, wherever money was wagered there was always the risk of a dispute about who actually won, whether they had done so fairly, and if they had triumphed within the agreed rules. Also, and given the royal and other forms of patronage, the amount of prize money on offer in horse racing grew rapidly so that the sums involved were vast. As increasing numbers of the social elite engaged with horse racing, they wanted to be sure that their horses were being entered into fair races, and also that any bets they placed would not be lost to crooked practices. By the early 1700s the agreements as to the terms of any race, which ensured a degree of clarity in terms of betting and prizes, were ever more likely to take the form of legal documents. In 1752 a group of gentlemen, predominantly owners and trainers, met in a London tavern to agree rules to govern the races that took place in Newmarket. Over the ensuing decades the remit of this group, which had given itself the name of The Jockey Club, spread beyond Newmarket and began governing all aspects of horse racing in Britain.

It was a landmark moment in the development of modern sport, although none of the gentlemen probably appreciated it at the time: they had formed the first governing body in the history of sport. In 1770 the annually published *Racing Calendar* emerged, and was the official journal of The Jockey Club. Not only did it inform readers of results and future schedules, but was also used to publicize the rules and regulations of racing. Throughout the later decades of the 18th century and into the 19th horse racing boomed, with scores of towns and cities hosting regular meetings. To solve the problem of making a fair bet, the gentlemen of racing had formed a club which standardized the sport. It was an important modernizing and transformative moment, and one that would be followed many times in different sports and geographical settings in the decades ahead.

The game of cricket, a rural bat and ball game, had been first recorded in England in the early 17th century. Its development was disrupted during the years of the Civil War (1642–51) but its popularity grew rapidly at the end of the century. As with horse racing one of the great impulses behind the game appears to have been gambling, with heavy wagers being bet on the outcome of matches. Cricket was an unusual game in its class make-up as a team, with its multitude of positions and skills, could accommodate the gentlemen patrons of the game as well as the talented labourer. In the later 1600s many of the upper class patrons of cricket, who would play in the matches themselves, also hired good cricketers (often from their own workforce) and paid them to play.

As with horse racing, the need to standardize the rules of cricket so that the gambling appeared fair, drove the game to regularization. A fairly typical issue had reared its head in September 1718. A match between the London Club and the Rochester Punch Club had been arranged on the basis of an agreed wager. When the London club looked like winning the game, the Rochester players walked off the pitch in the hope the game would be declared null and void, and that they would therefore keep their wager money. The London Club took the matter to court, where it was ordered that the game be played to its completion. This was done the following summer, in July 1719. The London Club won, and secured its wager from the Rochester team. Having been dragged into such a dispute, the London Club became focused on the terms of any match before they would agree to play. In 1787 the London Club moved to a new pitch, which had been purchased on their behalf by Thomas Lord, and renamed themselves the Marylebone Cricket Club (MCC). The first match was announced in the *Morning Herald* which stated: 'A grand match will be played on Monday 21 May in the New Cricket Ground, the New Road, Mary-le-bone, between eleven Noblemen of the White Conduit Club and eleven Gentlemen of the County of Middlesex with two men given, for 500 guineas a side. The wickets to be pitched at ten o'clock, and the match to be played out.' The announcement said it all about the origins of cricket: noblemen playing gentlemen, on a working weekday, for a large sum of money.

While there had been other rules to govern the game of cricket in circulation prior to the establishment of the MCC, these were often localized and had not been applied universally. In 1788 the MCC produced its Code of Laws, which were published in the *London Chronicle* in July 1789. While it took the MCC rules time to spread so that they were commonly applied wherever the game was played, they were successfully disseminated and the rules became universally recognized. The MCC still holds the copyright to the laws of cricket, and while any contemporary changes are made in agreement with the International Cricket Council, the MCC and its home ground of Lord's remain the home of cricket.

In a similar vein to horse racing and cricket, the same process happened in another fast growing sport of the 18th century, golf. It is Scotland which is most widely recognized as the home of golf, a stick and ball game played over a number of holes that initially flourished in and around Edinburgh. Various clubs were formed in the first decades of the 1700s. Without their own course many Edinburgh clubs played on the Leith links, an open area of ground, which had five holes which were played twice. One such group, the Honourable Company of Edinburgh Golfers, was presented with a trophy by Edinburgh Town Council in 1744, to be awarded to the winner of an annual competition. Alive to the disputes which were common at the time, the Council demanded that they would only make the award of the trophy if the competition was played under agreed rules. The Honourable Company produced a set of 13 rules, and these became the basis for the future development of the game along commonly agreed lines. A decade later another club, the Society of St Andrew's Golfers, was formed in Fife. Sharing much of its membership with the Honourable Gentlemen, the St Andrew's Club took a hand in refining the rules of golf in 1775 and again in 1809. In 1834, and demonstrating the prestige of the game and the St Andrew's Club, King William IV became its patron. The club's name was changed to the Royal and Ancient Golf Club of St Andrews, and it has overseen the management of the rules of golf ever since.

In the arena of horse racing, cricket, and golf, rules and regulations to govern the sport emerged to allow fair competition. This in turn meant that any gambling associated with the sport, often the main reason behind the contest, appeared transparent. The introduction of rules, and the emergence of bodies such as The Jockey Club or the MCC to form and implement them, resulted in forms of sport that became standardized. Even during this earlier, pre-industrialized period, this standardization was important as it made watching the race or the match a more attractive proposition as people, especially when they were informed by press coverage of such events, had a more intuitive sense of what was happening.

A hugely popular sport of the pre-industrial period, and one that would continue to grow through the industrial revolution, and after, was boxing. It differs from horse racing, cricket, and golf in that it was an avowedly urban sport. While having the occasional gentleman fighter from the social elite (such as Lord Byron, who practised at John Jackson's boxing academy in London) it was a spectacle whose contestants were largely working class men hired as champions. These hired fighters represented a patron who wagered heavily on the outcome. Boxing or prize fighting, as it was often known, had become popular, particularly in London, from the 1720s. The fights were ungoverned by any rules, and were ostensibly events organized to facilitate gambling. The contests were hugely popular and garnered a good deal of elite patronage and support, including both King George I and George II, who regularly attended bouts. While the selection and employment of a fighter, in the form of their champion by patrons, would allow a contest to take place and wagers to be made, the lack of any rules often created confusion. Essentially a bout was declared over, and a victor proclaimed when the opposing fighter could no longer continue. Before that happened a fight could go on for a long time, sometimes hours, and the injuries received by the fighters, given that this was bare knuckle fighting, were often horrific.

One fighter who rose to prominence in the 1730s was Jack Broughton. His patron was the Duke of Cumberland, for whom Broughton won a considerable sum of money in the decade and a half he was unbeaten. In 1741 Broughton killed a man during a bout. His initial response to the tragedy was the decision to never fight again, but to his backers and patrons Broughton was too valuable an asset to have idle outside the ring. Broughton was convinced to return to the ring in 1743, but only on the condition that rules be introduced to boxing that would make the fights safer for the boxers. Broughton's Rules disallowed blows below the belt or when a man was on the ground, broke the fight into rounds which allowed the fighters a 30-second rest, and started each new round with the two boxers coming to a mark in the centre of the ring.

Broughton himself fought one fight too many. At the age of 46 he accepted a challenge on which Cumberland wagered £10,000. Broughton was defeated, and an outraged Cumberland campaigned to have prize fighting outlawed. Laws were passed soon after, and prize fighting driven underground. Without an effective law enforcement process (the Metropolitan Police Force wasn't formed in London until 1829), prize fighting did however continue in secret in venues outside city and town boundaries. Prize fighting is symbolic of the contradiction at the heart of social attitudes, especially from the new urban middle classes, towards sport. As cities grew rapidly in the late 18th and early 19th century (London, for example, grew from 700,000 people in 1750 to 1.65 million by 1831), so the fear, and actuality, of urban crime and disorder came to the fore. Events such as prize fights were, in such a context, problematic. They were illegal events, yet brought all kinds of people together in big crowds where gambling, drinking, and all manner of antisocial and criminal activities took place.

The reformist belief that certain types of sporting events brought together the wrong kinds of people, fuelled with ill intent, did much to shape the emergent sporting landscape. The sports of the

2. William Hogarth's *The Pit Ticket* (1759) depicts a cock fight. It captures the raucous atmosphere that accompanied such sports staged to facilitate gambling and the wide range of social classes that attended

urban and rural poor were seen as a particular danger. Games such as folk football were sites of potential disorder, while other activities including cock fighting were deemed cruel to animals and injurious to the morals of those in attendance (Figure 2). When the working classes engaged in sports and recreations that included drinking, violence, and gambling they were viewed as threatening by a growing majority in society that believed in a moral, evangelizing code that promoted clean living, self-improvement, and sobriety.

The British context

The move against the animal based sports of the working classes began in 1822 when Richard Martin passed a bill through the British Parliament that outlawed cruelty against animals. Included in his legislation was a curb on bear baiting and dog fighting. In London, where animal sports were most prevalent, the London Police Act of 1839 prohibited the fighting or baiting of lions, bears, badgers, cocks, dogs, and other animals. With the regularization of sport by governing bodies and the legal moves against animal sports, the age of rational recreation had begun.

The industrial and transport revolutions of the 19th century transformed Britain and ensured its position as a global power. The wholesale change to the way that society functioned also revolutionized sport. During the decades of industrialization the working hours of the masses became regularized and free, or non-work time, became fixed. The various Factory Acts of the 1840s and 1850s regulated working hours and, most crucially in the context of sport, the 1850 Factory Act gave all workers a half day on Saturday. Those workers also became urbanized in a fashion previously unknown, and the railway revolution of the mid-19th century afforded the opportunity for relatively cheap and efficient travel between towns and cities. These macro changes were significant in preparing the ground for the sporting revolution that would follow in the second half of the 19th century. Traditional pastimes such as folk football were out of tune with the disciplines of industrial work and the tight confines of the new urban spaces. Also, many of the traditional rural holidays that had previously been the days on which such games were played were no longer observed and had been replaced by a shorter list of newly regulated and legally sanctioned public holidays.

Leisure became an important aspect of the industrial world as employers and lawmakers began to understand that increased productivity and the moral duty of care owed to the workers were enhanced by time off and holidays. Industrialization and urbanization transformed the landscape beyond recognition, and spaces where games had previously been played, such as common land, were no longer available for leisure. As a result, sporting spaces had to become fixed sites which were owned by a club, where the game and the associated crowds could be controlled. Control of the public was a big issue in the 19th century and as elected local authorities took control of municipal areas, so they sought to police disorder and crime. They also began, as did the national government, controlling and regulating popular entertainment. The nation's police forces, all in place by mid-century, if variously equipped and small, were central to enforcing codes of behaviour on the public and the policing of recreation and sport was a key task.

Sport then, in its modern sense, was initially a product of the British industrial revolution. The changes of that period brought a mass population together in urban settings, where they had access to leisure time and a varying amount of expendable income. Traditional sports that were rough and tumble and drew large, potentially uncontrollable crowds had no place in the new regimented world of time and space that industry ushered in. The sporting prototype of the upper classes that had emerged in horse racing, cricket, and golf had signalled the future, and the rational and regulated model of rules, clubs, and governing bodies was applied to the emergent sports of the industrial era. Once developed, the industrial model of sport would be one that was driven, in part, by capitalism, and a selection of key sports, most notably soccer, would emerge as mass scale commercial activities.

Education

Crucially in the multifaceted genesis of modern sport, educational institutions, in the form of private schools and universities, played an important foundational role. In doing so they imbued sport with a set of values and expectations that have been at the core of societal understandings of it ever since. Private, or as they were known in Britain, public schools, were largely vicious, disorganized places at the close of the 18th century. Boys who attended the schools often had more power than the masters. Geographically isolated, each of the main public schools developed some form of ball game which was specific to themselves, and in the playing of those games the future leaders of Britain were said to have developed their sense of leadership and character. With the growth of a new industrial and professional class, who were eager to climb the social ladder, parents began sending their children to these schools which had previously been a bastion of the lower rungs of the landowning aristocracy.

With a rise in the number of boys boarding at these schools and the resulting increase in revenues, in an age of Victorian respectability and self-improvement, the schools had to change. A series of reforming headmasters, such as Thomas Arnold at Rugby School from 1828, wrested control of the schools back from the boys, instilled order, improved the curriculum, and embraced sport as a means of controlling the pupils and teaching them valuable life lessons. At Rugby School the sport that emerged in codified form was rugby, a handling and kicking game that also featured scrimmages of boys around the ball and regular hacking or the kicking of each other's shins to gain control of the play. The first rules were written by the boys of the school in 1845. At Eton College a different style of ball game emerged which had little handling and more kicking or passing of the ball. While the schools were geographically distant from each other, these local variants of football developed separately. With the spread of the railways, and the advent of inter-school competition, the individual forms of the games spread more widely, and common rules and styles of play were agreed on between schools prior to matches taking place.

Whatever the style of play in the schools, one thing was clear: sport was given meaning in these settings. Sport in the schools was not simply for fun, a mere leisure activity, but rather functioned as another lesson. Sport was imbued with a series of values, morals, and ethics. These were developed on the field of play and became the standard by which the British male should live his life in business, the military, the clergy, or in political service. Essentially sport was said to develop those skills that would produce the future leaders of Britain and its empire. In this vein sport provided a blueprint for how life should be lived. On the field of play manliness, loyalty, honour, and respect for the opponents were all valorized. Boys learned how to become men. They were to demonstrate physical courage and leadership, to understand the nature of teamwork, and to always work within, and respect, the rules. In all this sport became a byword for honesty and integrity, for strength and gallantry. It was a theme that dominated public school education, and would come to define what it meant to be a man beyond the walls and cloisters of the schools. The imagery of a moral code that was taught through games was so enduring that it became a constant trope in popular culture at the time, and in the decades that followed, when everything from boys comics (*Boy's Own Paper*, 1879–1967) through to novels (*Tom Brown's School Days*, 1857) and films (the playing of Quidditch in the various Harry Potter stories, 1997–2007) would all encode this version of the ideal type of the man who developed a heightened sense of sportsmanship through his schooling.

The football codes

The development of the separate styles of football codes obviously became an issue when boys from different schools went to university. Keen to play a game, but with various views on what the game actually was, university undergraduates began figuring out for themselves what the best compromise was and what game they should play. In 1846 a group of Cambridge University undergraduates met and agreed rules for a game of football that favoured kicking rather than handling the ball. The Cambridge rules proved popular, and as the graduates who had played under those rules dispersed across the country, so football clubs began to be formed adhering to the Cambridge version of the game. Once outside an educational setting the game spread rapidly, and in 1863 the Football Association (FA) was formed to nationally regulate the game of football or soccer. The Rugby School handling version, although not as popular, had also developed a following and clubs were also formed to play that code. In 1871, the Rugby Football Union was formed as the governing body of the handling game.

Schools and universities would prove equally important in spreading sport around the globe, and alumni would feature centrally in the creation of various sporting codes and national governing bodies. In the US the elite colleges, like the public schools in Britain, played local variants of ball games, some which only allowed kicking, and others that allowed for handling and scrimmaging. The games, prior to codification, were essentially mob games not unlike folk football. In Princeton their game was known as ballown, while in Harvard a mob ball game, known as Bloody Monday and begun in 1827, was a match between freshmen and sophomores. At Dartmouth the game was Old Division Football, the rules of which were published in 1871, and was a kicking game between two teams of unlimited size. In the late 1860s and early 1870s regular intercollegiate contests began to be staged. One of the first was the contest between Rutgers and Princeton played in 1869. The rules were fixed by the home college, and for each match the away team had to adapt to unfamiliar rules. Other colleges joined these contests, and an annual fixture list of intercollegiate games emerged.

With regular contests the need for standard rules emerged. The challenge was how to bring together colleges playing a handling and scrimmaging game, with those who favoured a kicking game. The compromises of the 1873–80 period led to the standardization of rules and the emergence of a specifically American game. The first meetings to standardize rules in 1873 were attended by Yale, Columbia, Princeton, and Rutgers, but their rules dealt with a kicking game. Harvard refused to attend as they favoured a handling game. After spreading the gospel of what was essentially the rugby code, Harvard brought together Yale, Princeton, Columbia, and themselves to agree a standard set of rules for a rugby styled game in 1876. Walter Camp, a Yale student, attended the 1880 meeting of the footballing colleges and began suggesting various changes to the game, such as reducing the number of players, creating a line of scrimmage, and reducing the size of the pitch. In introducing the changes Camp was trying to create a much faster game where speed was more important than strength. His changes moved the game away from its rugby styled roots, and created American football. The game grew quickly, and between 1880 and 1900 the number of colleges playing the American game of football had increased from 8 to 43.

Back in Britain the development of two main football codes, soccer and rugby, was marked in large part by class. The first years of soccer were driven by an enthusiasm for the game amongst those who had brought it into being, namely ex-public school boys. They dominated the early years of the Football Association, and also formed the bulk of the various teams that won competitions in the early years. With the broader changes in society caused by the industrial revolution and Britain's manufacturing and imperial wealth, the working classes were finding time for leisure. In soccer they found the perfect game: something that required little in the way of facilities or equipment, whose rules were simple, and which did not require complex training or preparation. The growth of soccer in Britain was staggering. Eight years after the founding of the FA it had 50 affiliated clubs. Three decades later, by 1900, the number of clubs that had joined the FA exceeded 10,000. Clubs were formed by informal groups of workers while others were organized as factory teams and funded by the employers. Church groups and social associations were other places where clubs were founded, and many public houses and hotels also joined the fray. The spread of soccer was also signified by a rapid national expansion. This was not the game of a particular region, but rather one that was diffused throughout the north of England, into Scotland, across the Midlands and the south.

The massive and rapid expansion of soccer, often dubbed the game of the people and applauded for its democratic nature, was due to the advent of free time, the support of tram and railway companies who moved players and supporters from town to town on match day, and the simple fact that it was proving hugely popular to play and to watch. Soccer attracted people through the turnstiles and made money. It also attracted the support and backing of the commercial classes who assisted in the founding of clubs. They invested their money into what they primarily saw, no matter what their affection for the game, as a financial opportunity. In this, soccer shifted from its elite, public school roots, into a game played by the workers, but administered by industrialists. Initially soccer fixtures had revolved around challenge matches that were set up locally. The rapid spread of the game led to the suggestion that a challenge cup, which would be open to all members of the FA, be offered. The first competitive matches in the FA Cup were duly played in November 1871. There appeared no limit to the appeal of the game or the cup, and in the quest to ensure a high number of regular fixtures (and income), 12 professional teams agreed in 1888 to form the Football League. With the workers of Britain free from their employment by 2 p.m. on Saturday, that afternoon became the day for soccer, and purpose built stadia were packed with thousands watching their local team. While cricket remained the dominant and most popular game for the summer, it was soccer, a sport that had emerged free of socially elite control, that found its following, and its players, in the heartlands of working class industrial Britain during the winter months.

Baseball

In soccer Britain found its national game: a sport that was made professional early on, and whose clubs were owned as profit making entities and not as private clubs for the enjoyment and entertainment of an elite. In the US, the elite colleges favoured their own form of football, and this remained an amateur sport with a specific class dynamic until the turn of the 20th century. The first national game in the US was baseball. It has been argued that the roots of the game can be found in some form of compromise between the British games of rounders and cricket, and the local stick and ball games of cat and town ball. The recognized roots of baseball were in New York in the form of Alexander Cartwright, who wrote the first rules of baseball for his club, the Knickerbockers in 1845. As with the development of sports in Britain, the thrust of Cartwright's rule writing was to create a standardized game so that when challenges were made with other teams there were no arguments as to what style of game was to be played. Forms of baseball were popular in the north-east by the mid-19th century, and the new rules served to bolster the appeal of the game (Figure 3). Sixteen clubs met in 1857 to further revise Cartwright's rules, and a year later a challenge match between the clubs of New York and those of Brooklyn drew a crowd of 4,000.

Sports are diffused from their points of origin in many different ways, and in the US it was the Civil War (1861–5) that transformed the geographical focus of baseball from a sport that was regional

3. Crowds gathered to watch a professional baseball game (*c.*1910). The wooden stands and perimeter fences, as well as the attendant police officer, exist to control and regulate the paying crowd

to one that was national. The diffusion can be charted in the membership of the first organizing body of the game, the National Association of Base Ball Players, which had been founded in New York in 1857. At the end of the Civil War 100 clubs were affiliated to the National Association. With the return to peace, the game thrived, and a decade later the list of affiliated clubs had grown to over 400 clubs, including ones on the west coast and in the south.

Once established as a national game, and with clubs backed by investors looking to attract crowds, baseball turned professional. In the winter of 1868 professionalism in the game was accepted by the National Association, and at the start of the 1869 season 12 clubs had declared themselves professional. With outgoing wages, and stands to fill, the owners of clubs needed regular fixtures to ensure (or at least try and achieve) profitability. The first attempt at a major league ran from 1871 to 1875, but was replaced by the National Base Ball League in 1876. The National League was the brainchild of the businessman, and an official of the Chicago White Stockings, William Hulbert. The National League was conceived as an organization that would serve the interests of the clubs and its owners above those of the players, and exert a powerful central influence over the game. Its authority would be challenged by the players and also by competing leagues in its early decades, but despite this the National League survived. In conjunction with the American League from 1901, the National League created a nationwide schedule of play, and a network of city based clubs. By the outbreak of the First World War professional baseball would be staging over 1,000 games a season and attracting average crowds of around 4,000 paying spectators.

Global diffusion

Sport would be diffused well beyond the major cities of Britain and the US. The reach of Britain, and its trading and administrative machinery, criss-crossed the globe between its formal and informal empires, while US cultural and capital power also moved around the world. New Zealand took up rugby from the 1870s and the game came to dominate the national psyche. The game spread beyond the elite and captivated the native Maori population so that the game became, and remains, the definition of what it means to be a Kiwi. Cricket was recorded in the country from the 1830s and 1840s, and became the dominant summer game. Soccer has always occupied a lesser place in the nation's affections, and while a national association was founded in 1891, the game relied on pockets of population in urban and industrial centres for its support. In South Africa the British army was initially the major agency of diffusion of sporting culture, but it was in the elite universities of Cape Town and Stellenbosch that rugby prospered. The class and race dynamics of South Africa had a defining impact on sport there. Soccer, a game favoured by working class Britons in the army, was a game that proved popular amongst the local black population. In the late 19th and early 20th century any mixing of the races on the sporting field was untenable, and the white British settler population, joined by the local Afrikaners, embraced rugby as their game. The sport, and to a lesser extent cricket, became the definer of South African sporting identity in the apartheid years. Soccer was the preserve of the black population, and in the years since democratic rule was introduced the game has prospered with South Africa hosting the 2010 World Cup. As David Goldblatt stated, soccer in South Africa functioned as 'an instrument of social organization, cultural self-expression and a yard stick for demonstrating the limits and fragilities of the colonizing authorities'.

Australia is often viewed as a sport obsessed nation where national success, on various fields of play, do more to define nationality than any other cultural sphere. Australia was the most British of colonies and the games of home were readily transplanted by those who settled there. Cricket was first recorded in 1803, and the first rugby club founded at Sydney University in 1864. In 1859, in an attempt to keep cricket players fit during the winter, a new game was invented, namely Australian Rules football, which came to dominate the state of Victoria and went professional from the 1880s. Soccer arrived in the 1870s, but failed to compete with the major sports until it grew in the post-Second World War years with a major influx of population from Greece, Italy, Yugoslavia, and other parts of Europe.

On the Indian subcontinent it was the British civil service and the army that provided the sporting evangelists. Soccer arrived in 1854, and a Football Association formed in 1893. The game was the preserve of the ranks of the British army and regimental teams played regular competitions. In Bengal soccer proved popular amongst the local population, albeit played for its own nationalist reasons. In 1911, the local team Mohun Bagan famously defeated the East Yorkshire Regiment in a challenge match in front of 60,000 people. However, it wasn't soccer that would become the defining sport in India, but cricket. First played by sailors of the East India Company in 1721, cricket was endorsed by the colonial elite and mobilized as a vehicle to co-opt the upper echelons of Indian society into supporting British rule and culture. The Viceroy of India, Lord Curzon, wanted the Indians to adopt British culture and his rallying call, issued in 1899, included the demand that they take to manly sports and games. As with many other nations of empire, India had seen the establishment of elite schools in the 1860s and 1870s and, as had happened in Britain, these became the starting point of a wide diffusion of the game of cricket, and its associated ethic, across Indian society. The process was so successful, that in the years after decolonization and the creation of Pakistan and Bangladesh, it was cricket that became the premier game of the subcontinent. Given the population sizes of the three countries, and the emergent wealth of India in recent decades, they now form the most powerful bloc in world cricket. The 2011 clash between India and Pakistan was watched by an estimated television audience of 1 billion people, and the Indian

Premier League Cricket tournament is now the wealthiest cricket tournament in the world with Pepsi paying $65 million in sponsorship in a three-year deal from 2013.

Across the formal British Empire, the spread of sport can be understood as a product of cultural imperialism, the transplantation of its educational system, the ready movement of large numbers of Britons to the various colonies, and the constantly renewing population of British civil servants, police officers, military men, entrepreneurs, and speculators who took their games with them and used them as a means of meeting, on common ground, with the local population. The process across Britain's informal empire was different. Less the product of direct colonial control and presence, and assisted by migrant populations, traders, and imperial adventurers from other European nations, sport was diffused across oceans and boundaries through constant travelling from home to countries across the globe whose populations would witness, share, and then adapt sport for their own purposes.

In South America, Europeans were central to the industries associated with the exploitation of natural resources and the building of the necessary transport links to move goods. From the 1860s Britons and other Europeans were present in South America in large numbers. The British population of Buenos Aires in 1880 numbered 40,000, and sport was central to their social life. Clubs were established for rugby, cricket, and soccer, and a network of British inspired schools proselytized the games ethic. The first soccer game was played in Argentina in 1867, and from 1891 a national league founded. In Uruguay, a Scottish schoolteacher, William Leslie Poole, started a cricket club in 1891 and a soccer team in 1893, with a city wide league for Montevideo formed in 1901. In Brazil, Charles Miller, a member of São Paulo Athletic Club, who had been sent to England for his education, returned home in 1894 with two soccer balls.

He spread the game through his own club and on to a network of work based clubs. Joined eventually by German immigrant adherents of the game, São Paolo had a city league by 1902. Following the establishment of the game of soccer in various South American nations in the last decades of the 19th century, the game was indigenized in the years to the outbreak of the First World War, with a network of clubs being formed that spurned connections with the foreign, English speaking elite. In the inter-war years national federations were set up across Central and South America, and the rapid population growth in urban centres led to a boom in soccer based around workplace teams. The success of the game of soccer in the region was evidenced by the staging of the first World Cup finals in Uruguay in 1930. Thirteen teams took part, seven of which were from South America, and Uruguay were the champions, defeating Argentina in front of 93,000 spectators.

Sport also developed across continental Europe in the 19th century, and what emerged was a mix between adaptations of the British model (team sports such as soccer and rugby), and the codification of many traditional pastimes. In Germany, for example, there was a definite attempt to resist the spread of British team sports as they were seen as un-German. What was favoured instead was the Turnen form of gymnastics, which was centred in ideals of exercise and bodily control. Turnen and other forms of gymnastics were powerful forces across Europe in the late 19th century and the dominance of the practice is evidenced by the move of Turnen to the United States with emigrant Europeans. The Nordic countries offer another model, which is referred to as *idrott*, meaning any athletic activity that uses physical skill. In the Nordic countries there was a rich diet of traditional and highly localized games, which were mixed, especially in the rising urban areas, with imported sports such as soccer, new games like team handball, and traditional winter activities such as skiing, which were made competitive and codified.

Across Europe physical education through gymnastics primarily was a far more powerful force than it was in Britain, and this culture meant that sport did develop differently. Although team sports such as soccer would come to dominate across Europe, sport as a physical activity that was linked to conceptions of the nation and strength was a powerful force. This can be observed in the inter-war years when a plethora of political movements (both left and right) and the fascist regimes in Germany, Italy, Spain, and Portugal, as well as the communists of the Soviet Union, all promoted sport as an activity that encapsulated strength and beauty. While these regimes were happy to engage with team sports (Mussolini was particularly keen to capitalize on the success of the Italian soccer team after they won the 1938 World Cup final), the strong tradition of gymnastics meant that all these political movements favoured bodily training and physical control. Sport in this context was a stage for the preparation of the body for military service, and also a vehicle through which the regime could prove its ideological superiority by defeating other nations in a host of different sports.

The emergence of the US as a world power from the late 19th century led to the dispersal of that nation's chosen sports. In areas where the US had military, economic, or cultural interests the outward flow of sports, as happened with earlier European colonial enterprises, took place. Baseball was spread to Central America and certain Caribbean islands. The game was supported by the widely contrasting figures of Rafael Trujillo, right wing dictator of the Dominican Republic, and Cuba's leftist leader, Fidel Castro, who both ensured the game became popular in their countries. In Mexico the first games of baseball were played in the 1880s and it quickly moved beyond the resident American population to become popular amongst urban Mexicans. By 1904 a semi-professional league had been established, and by 1925 a fully professional league. The vibrancy of baseball as the leading game in the region, and the skill of the players, led US Major League Baseball (MLB) teams to see the area as a talent pool that could be tapped. In 1956 the first Dominican, Ozzie Virgil, was signed to the New York Giants, and he has been followed by hundreds more. Currently 30 MLB teams run talent camps in the Dominican Republic, and being successfully signed is seen as one route out of an economically underdeveloped nation. The value of making it in US baseball is clear. In 2012 the average wage in the Dominican Republic was just less than $500, whereas the average of wage of the MLB players who represented the Dominican Republic at the 2013 World Baseball Classic was $5.2 million.

Baseball was introduced to Japan in 1878 by a returning railway worker who had learnt the game while studying in the US. The game there was supported early on by the MLB, and the first Japanese League was established in 1936. Baseball became popular in Taiwan during the period of the Japanese occupation during the Second World War, and has since become a symbol of sporting resistance, a national game, in the face of Chinese control. In Japan baseball has had to compete with soccer. A professional soccer league was established in 1993, and in 2002 the staging of the World Cup (jointly hosted with South Korea) was a huge success.

The Asian nations offer a good example of how the flow of sport is not simply out from the west. Across the Asian world there are a series of sports, broadly characterized as martial arts, which have records that date back to a period between the 6th and 10th centuries. While the growth of trading and political links with the west in the 19th century took sports into Asia, it also allowed for the spread of martial arts and the associated cultural practices in the other direction. Edward Barton-Wright, a railway engineer who had been working in Japan, is credited with bringing jujitsu to Britain in the 1890s where he would eventually establish a school of martial arts. A range of martial arts spread across the western world in the 20th century and in addition to those fighting styles, more meditative bodily practices such as yoga also became part of the western sporting landscape.

Resistance

While sport was spread across the world in many different ways and by a plethora of agencies, the history of sport is not solely the story of dominant global games which had British origins. In a similar vein to the US rejection of cricket and rugby in favour of baseball and American football, so other nations resisted. In Canada the copies of elite British schools led to a mid-19th century flourish of cricket, but this was quickly exchanged for baseball from the neighbouring US. Lacrosse was popular in Canadian universities, but again the pull of near neighbours, in the form of the American colleges who were embracing their own form of football, led to the creation in 1891 of the Canadian Football Union. Soccer was brought to Canada by emigrant Britons, but the game struggled to find a foothold and it was ice hockey, a game suited to the long winters and that could be played by all ages and classes, that took hold. The game was codified in 1877 by students at McGill University, and by the early 1890s there were over 100 clubs in Montreal. Enclosed rinks were built across Canada, and elsewhere in North America. By the turn of the century clubs were employing professional players, and in 1910 the game came under a national regulatory body in the form of the National Hockey Association which, by 1917, had been renamed the National Hockey League and enlarged to include professional teams from the US.

In China the early entry of western sport under the auspices of the YMCA waned after the First World War. In the decades of upheaval that were to follow, including the anti-sport years of the Cultural Revolution, China appeared, in western terms, a sporting backwater. Since the 1970s Chinese attitudes towards sport have changed and what was often seen as an eastern resistance to the appeal of organized western sports has collapsed. Soccer was embraced, and a professional league has been in place since 1993. In a similar way to the Soviets before them the Chinese realized that victories on the world stage were beneficial to their national well-being. Chinese athletes began winning, and at the Olympics were dominant in areas such as women's swimming and gymnastics. The staging of the Beijing Olympics in 2008 symbolized a new openness from China and was also seen to represent the nation's economic miracle and sporting prowess.

In Ireland, despite its geographical closeness to Britain, and the initial success through to the 1880s of British forms of sport, there was a nationalistically informed rejection of what were called foreign games, namely soccer, rugby, cricket, and hockey. Cricket was the most popular game in the country prior to the establishment of the Gaelic Athletic Association (GAA) in 1884. The foundation of the GAA was driven by the desire of Irish cultural nationalists to produce a game that was not a function of British colonialism. In inventing Gaelic football and hurling, the Association created the two most popular games on the island of Ireland, and ones that speak to a culturally indigenous form of sport as opposed to one that was diffused from the imperial centre. They are games that remain amateur, are community based, and offer a sporting definition of Irishness. The contemporary success of the GAA, in the face of competition from Premier League soccer and other leisure pursuits, is a testament to the founding vision of the Association and is a game that still draws a crowd in excess of 80,000 to its annual finals in September every year.

The last decades of the 19th century were ones of huge innovation and social change across a range of areas. Sport was a by-product of the industrial, transport, and urbanizing revolutions of the period. Once codified, rationalized, and organized, sports were dispersed on the lines of travel that linked cities with towns, colonies with the home nation, and marketplaces with the suppliers of raw materials. Various games were commercialized

4. Edith Parker playing tennis in Chicago (1903). Parker was a leading American player at the turn of the century, and the physicality of her approach to the game marked a switch from women's sedate enjoyment of a leisure pursuit to their participation in a competitive sport

and professionalized, but in all the changes and transformations as sport modernized and spread, key foundation ethics remained at the heart of what was meant and embodied by playing sport (Figure 4).

Chapter 3
Amateurs and professionals

Most surveys carried out in the western world currently suggest that nearly half of people over the age of 16 take part in some form of sporting or physical activity every week. While there are always concerns that this figure should be higher, given the health and wellness benefits of physical exercise, it is worth remembering that all but the tiniest fraction of those who do play sport each week, do so for their own intrinsic gain, and will receive no monetary reward for their participation. So, while much of the analysis, history, and commentary about the role of sport in societies across the world focuses on the elite professional, those few who are paid to play are the exception rather than the rule. The vast majority of people who play sport are amateurs who take part for a variety of reasons relating to their social lives, health, and for the pure pleasure of it.

Amateurism

The definition of an amateur emerged in the 19th century and spoke of someone who cultivated anything as a pastime, as distinguished from one who prosecuted it professionally. In its broadest sense, the moniker amateur was also often used in a disparaging manner, denoting someone who dabbled in an activity or undertook it in a superficial way. But in the sporting world the term had a much more robust meaning, and certainly did not dismiss the amateur as a dabbler. In 1882, for example, the sporting newspaper, *The Field*, in a debate over the pay for play issue warned that players should either keep 'within the bounds of honest amateurism, or turn professional'. In this amateurism was given value: it was honest, whereas professionalism was something altogether different. If players were paid their motivation for taking part in sport shifted away from a moral sense of the values and meanings of sport to one where they were simply motivated by their remuneration and would transgress the rules and spirit of the game accordingly.

The gentlemen who acted as the creators of modern sport in the 19th century, whether in schools, colleges, clubs, or regulating bodies, were all driven by the principle that the games they were organizing should be amateur. The core values of sporting amateurism, its codes, have been outlined many times by historians of the period, but they can be summed up as leisure, loyalty, and decency pursued by gentlemen. Caught up in these blanket ideals were the specific beliefs that sport should inculcate in its players a respect for the order of rules, the leadership of the captain, the belief in fair play, and the tying together of mind and soul in the practice of muscular Christianity. Or as Richard Holt surmised, 'Sport was not just about winning and losing: it was a moral and aesthetic endeavour. How you played the game was all important.'

The values given to sport were part of education, and were ones learnt and practised on the field of play that would then be transferred as guiding principles for life. It has been rightly argued that the creation of the amateur sporting ethos protected the individual and the group from the market and the state. Thus, while sport and its values assisted in creating the ideal Victorian male who would serve society, the actual practice of sport, the bedrock of Victorian decency, was something that had to be kept separate from the potentially immoral world of commerce. Sport was conceived, in principle at least, as something pure. The vision of 19th century amateur sport was also one which was entirely masculine. Those men who created modern sport, who tied together ancient Greek sporting idealism with the rough and tumble of ball games, believed that society lacked something beyond industrial wealth and Enlightenment reason. Essentially the sporting reformers wanted to see medieval chivalry recreated in modern sportsmanship, and as a result a valorized form of upright masculinity was hard-wired into the very origins of modern, codified sport.

Clearly the link between amateurism as an ethos, and the playing of sport, was a product of British conditions, but was also recognized and celebrated by others elsewhere such as Pierre de Coubertin, the founder of the modern Olympic Games or those who would formalize college athletics in the US. The argument wasn't simply about payment for play, but rather the protection of the amateur as someone who stood for a clearly outlined set of values. Money was, put simply, a corrupting force. Clearly some sports such as rugby battled hard to retain full amateurism, others like cricket adapted a halfway house approach, while the game of soccer professionalized rapidly. The key point here however is not necessarily the historical detailing of which sports embraced full or partial pay for play, but rather that the amateur ethos, as opposed to the amateur status of not receiving pay, was carried through all sports. It is sportsmanship and fair play which are the key legacies of the 19th century originators of sport, and which still maintain a powerful hold over how we expect athletes to conduct themselves.

Amateur and professional divisions

It would be professional, or at least commercialized sport, that emerged stronger than the unpaid, amateur version. Sports which had organized themselves in the 18th century, such as horse racing, cricket, golf, and boxing, had all accepted the principle that certain people, whether trainers, jockeys, caddies, players, and fighters, could be remunerated for their labours. In many popular urban sports, such as pedestrianism or foot racing, tracks were built alongside public houses, and entrance fees charged for spectators to watch the contests. On New Year's Day 1848, for instance, at Belle Vue in Manchester, 10,000 people paid threepence each to watch a series of foot races and sprints. Much mid-19th century sport was commercial, and it was against such commercialism, with its attendant drinking and gambling, that the amateur lobby would mount their campaign of sporting purity.

The most telling example of the clash between the views of amateurs and the professionals, who were a product of the commercialization of sport, happened in the game of rugby. The sport had been codified at Rugby School (1845), and proved popular in other elite schools and colleges. It had spread beyond its initial demographic of the social elite, and had found a popular following in the industrial towns of the north of England amongst the sport hungry workers. The governing body of the game, the Rugby Football Union (RFU), was dominated by the southern, socially elite followers of the game who had an unswerving commitment to amateurism. In the north, the game flourished and brought in large crowds who watched competitions such as the Yorkshire Cup, which was started in 1877 as a challenge tournament for local clubs. However, despite the commercialization of the game in terms of paying crowds, the amateur rules of the RFU forbade any player being paid broken time payments for missing work so that they could play. In 1893 the Yorkshire clubs had asked the RFU to allow broken time payments, but that proposal was rejected. Frustrated and angry at the inability of the RFU to understand the predicament of northern working class players, the clubs of Lancashire and Yorkshire agreed, in August 1895, to resign from the RFU. They established a new union, the Northern Rugby Football Union, which would allow players to be paid. In the course of just over a decade the Northern Union altered the rules of the rugby union game, and by 1907 was not only professional, but was playing an entirely separate rugby code, namely rugby league. The split in rugby over the very issue of pay for play was mirrored in New Zealand in 1907, New South Wales, Australia, in 1907, and in Queensland in 1908. In each case a professional league broke away from the national or regional rugby union authorities which would not countenance the idea of paid players.

The split in rugby over pay for play was a microcosm of the larger issues between amateurs and professionals. The former didn't simply oppose the idea of payment for players, but argued that the accompanying commercialization of sport and the shift in player motivation and ethos altered the very moral grounds on which sport was played. It was also simple snobbery, and a desire amongst the social elite to keep their games free of the lower orders. The separate social spheres for the classes were most pronounced in cricket (Figure 5). While the game had allowed for the payment of players very early on, it was also a game at the administrative level, and in the manner in which it was played, that spoke to a particular amateur ethos. To underline the class distinctions in cricket the amateurs were referred to as gentlemen, had separate dressing rooms, and entered the field of play by a separate gate to the professionals, who were known as players. In England one of the amateur players was always the captain of the side. It took until 1952 before the English national team employed a professional captain, and until 1962 before the amateur status was abolished. The distinction was not evident in Australia where, from an early period, the players, whatever their social status, commonly shared a proportion of the gate money between them. By the time of Australian cricket's golden age, from the 1890s to the outbreak of the First World War, playing for a fee, effectively professionalism, was the norm.

Where the amateur–professional split was most closely mirrored outside England was in the Caribbean, India, and South Africa, but these distinctions had more to do with

5. The cricketers C. B. Fry and Ranjitsinhji, the Maharaja Jam Sahib
of Nawanagar (1905). Both men were amateurs and played cricket
together for Sussex and England. Fry was the great all rounder of his
era, and also represented England in soccer and equalled the long
jump record of the period

colonial period race issues than class. Cricket was a game which the white colonists—civil servants, military officers, and missionaries—shared with the social elites and ruling classes in many countries. The place of the game as a symbol of social elitism was reinforced by its presence on the curriculum of a series of local copies of English public schools such as Presidency College in Calcutta, Harrison College in Barbados, and Grey College in Bloemfontein, amongst others. Patronage of the game, as a way of creating shared elite colonial and indigenous spaces was also a common feature of the development of the game as with Lord Harris's Presidency matches (Europeans versus Parsees from 1892) and Malcolm Hailey, the Governor of Punjab's Governor's XI versus The Rest. In the Caribbean the history and meanings of cricket, particularly in a race, nation, and empire setting were brilliantly recorded in C. L. R. James's *Beyond A Boundary* (1963). James shows how the game came to the Caribbean, and how race and class combined to create a multi-layered game. One was the preserve of a colonial and local elite (and again prestigious local schools played a big part in sustaining such distinctions), while the other was a popular game of the parishes of the various islands, and played by everyone. The amateur–professional divide fell, as it did in many parts of the British Empire, along lines of class and colour: whites and the local social elite were amateurs, the indigenous played professionally.

The representative team of the Caribbean, the West Indies, symbolizes the struggle. Led by C. L. R. James, then editor of *The Nation* newspaper, nationalists seeking island independence rallied to the cause of a black, professional captain for the team. Between 1957 and 1960 the captain chosen by the selectors was the white wicket keeper, Gerry Alexander. Alexander was a graduate of Jamaica's elite Wolmer's Boy's School and Cambridge University. He played for Cambridge in both cricket and soccer, eventually representing Great Britain in amateur soccer before returning to the Caribbean and playing 25 times for the West Indies cricket team. Alexander led a talented team that included three iconic black players, Frank Worrell, Everton Weekes, and Clyde Walcott. C. L. R. James offered the opinion in 1958, when Alexander was selected as captain, that it was revolting that Alexander would be the leader of a team in which the exceptionally skilled Walcott was playing. The campaign against the white amateur captaincy was eventually successful and in 1961 Walcott led the team on a tour to Australia as captain.

In the US the professional–amateur question was not a major issue in the main commercialized sports. In baseball professional players held sway from the 1870s, in football the first professional league was formed in 1902, ice hockey followed two years later, and it was the ice hockey team owners, looking to maximize the usage of their stadia, that brought the professional basketball league into being in 1946. Sport in the US was driven by commercial concerns, and the need for owners to maximize their profits. While this situation made professionalism possible very early on in the development of each of the main US sports, it has also created tension. The owners of sports clubs, in all the main sports, were a powerful cartel who operated together in an attempt to control player movement and to restrict their freedom in terms of their contracts and salary. This has led to far more disputes, strikes, and lockouts between owners and players in US sport than elsewhere in the world as the players sought a higher share of income and profits. Despite the avowed commercialism and professionalism of these US games from an early stage, the regulatory bodies of each expected that the values of fair play, respect for the opposition, and an adherence to the rules would inform the conduct of the paid players.

The NCAA

Given the close relationship of the US to market liberalism, a force which its professional sports leagues have reflected very powerfully, the country is also home to the most tightly controlled and rigorously policed amateur sporting organization in the contemporary world: the National Collegiate Athletic Association (NCAA). College athletics emerged in the second half of the 19th century and proved very popular with spectators. The spectacle of intercollegiate contests drew big crowds, and many of the leading colleges began to see commercial benefits from staging sporting events, in particular football. Despite the success of sport in the college environment, there was significant opposition. Charles William Eliot, the President of Harvard from 1869, opposed football, hockey, and basketball in the college setting, and noted that gate receipts from games had turned amateur contests into major commercial spectacles. Eliot went so far as to try and abolish football at Harvard arguing that it was violent, and because rule breaking had become the norm as teams sought a competitive advantage, believed the whole exercise was morally corrupt.

The issue that forced the formation of the NCAA was the violence inherent in football. In 1905 alone, 18 deaths and over 100 serious injuries were recorded in college football. Such was the level of concern that President Roosevelt organized a meeting of college leaders at the White House to discuss the problems facing football. The meeting was followed by a further gathering of college officials in New York to establish clearer and safer rules for football and, on 28 December 1905, the formation of the intercollegiate Athletic Association of the United States of America, which would then change its name to the NCAA in 1910. At the heart of the NCAA's rule book was a commitment to amateurism. The argument was straightforward: all college athletes were ultimately attending university to gain a degree, and any commitment to sport must be a secondary concern to education. Through to the 1950s, despite the amateurism of the student athletes, colleges treated sport as a business opportunity and a way to generate income and boost their profile. The practices relating to the recruitment of players were questioned and the financial aid offered to student athletes was, in certain cases, going above and beyond the normal level of a scholarship.

To rectify the situation, especially significant with the advent of television and the additional riches that might bring, the NCAA appointed a permanent Executive Director in 1951 and established its first national headquarters in Kansas City.

Over the decades the NCAA regulated the relationship between college sports and television, and created a multi-division structure so that colleges could be pooled with others of similar resource bases. Television made the NCAA rich. In the first year of coverage in 1952, NBC paid $1 million to screen 11 football games. In a period of growth the NCAA completely ignored women's sport. In 1971 the Association of Intercollegiate Athletics for Women (AIAW) was founded to support women's athletics. At the time women athletes at top division sport colleges received only 2 per cent of the athletics budget. In 1972, the passage of Title XI legislated for equal access to education and outlawed discrimination within the educational setting. In sport the legislation meant that colleges had to provide for women's sport on their campuses in the same way they provided for the male equivalent. The NCAA resisted the legislation, and argued that revenue generating sports, namely football and basketball, should be exempt. They attempted to defend their position in court, but lost. Since the early 1980s the NCAA took over the women's remit of the AIAW and has since fully administered women's sport at the national level (Figure 6). Women athletes are bound by the same amateur rules as their male counterparts, but despite any advances made under Title XI it is still the revenue generating sports that are most valorized by colleges and most sought after by those media companies buying television rights.

The NCAA has become a very powerful and wealthy sports organization within the US. At the end of 2012 it had recorded a revenue for the year of $871 million. The same is true for the top sports colleges who spend millions of dollars ensuring that their programmes are successful. The argument is made that team sports on campus create school spirit, maintain concrete links

6. Teresa Weatherspoon was one of the players who competed in the inaugural season of the professional Women's National Basketball Association in 1997, playing for New York Liberty. She played in every game, in each season, from 1997 to 2003, before returning to her alma mater, Louisiana Tech, to join the coaching staff

with alumni who will financially commit to the college, and give the institution a high media profile. In 2012 the top three spending colleges on their athletics programmes were Texas ($138 million), Ohio State ($124 million), and Michigan ($115 million). For these three the profit from their programmes amounted to approximately $20 million. Many colleges outside the top few actually subsidize their athletics programmes and they are a drain on resources. For the top teams, usually in men's football or basketball teams, the salaries paid to coaches are comparable with top professional leagues around the world. In 2013, the Alabama coach, Nick Saban, had an annual salary estimated at $5.5 million. In the same year the coach of the English national soccer team, Roy Hodgson, earned $4.5 million.

The NCAA has become one the staunchest defenders of amateurism in the contemporary world, and yet as a business its income and expenditure model (with the exception of player salaries) differs little to the NFL (National Football League) or the English Premier League. And in its three key sports, men's football, basketball, and ice hockey, the NCAA and the colleges feed their best athletes direct into the professional game. As a result of the money within college sports, and the close relationship to professional sports, there have been transgressions of the NCAA's amateur rules, and there is a body of opinion that argues that a 19th century ideal, even in the world of the student athlete, is no longer fit for purpose. The argument that education comes first and sport second is, in most colleges in the top NCAA divisions, nonsense. While three-quarters of white student athletes manage to graduate, the figure for black athletes across the US averages barely half. And research that concluded in 2010 showed that 8 per cent of athletes at the University of North Carolina were functionally illiterate and 60 per cent had reading levels that were between fourth and eighth grade. So while the NCAA still defines sportsmanship as exhibiting behaviours that are based on such fundamental values as respect, fairness, civility, honesty, and responsibility, it oversees a structure of athlete recruitment which is open to abuse when enticements are offered, it fails to ensure that the majority of student athletes graduate (or in some cases can even read and write), and it favours specific revenue raising male sports above the rest.

The end of amateurism?

In the last decades of the 20th century one international sport, rugby union, and one global sporting organization, the International Olympic Committee (IOC), were still resistant, along with the NCAA, to the force of professionalism. The game of rugby union had blocked any moves towards professionalism throughout the 20th century, but in the 1990s, the availability of ever increasing sums of television money brought into open debate the amateur status of the game. Many players around the world in the early 1990s complained that they were training and competing as professionals, but were not being paid for their services. This despite a network of national leagues, international competition, and, since 1987, the start of the Rugby World Cup which meant that the top players were committed to long seasons of training and playing. In Australia and New Zealand there was an alternative to players as the rugby league's Super League had signed a major television deal and was able to entice top union players to the professional game. To combat the threat from rugby league, the rugby unions of Australia, South Africa, and New Zealand agreed to sign up with Rupert Murdoch's News Corporation, a deal worth $550 million over a decade, and play a tri-nation provincial competition known as the Super 12. The wealth of the deal meant that the three southern hemisphere unions were challenging the amateur rule.

The sense of frustration amongst northern hemisphere players was best expressed by the then England captain, Will Carling. During the run-up to the 1995 World Cup an English rugby administrator, Dudley Wood, had argued that the English player's desire to win was leading them to cheat, and such behaviour was in contravention to the amateur ethic. Carling responded by dismissing the leadership of English rugby as '57 old farts'. The comment led to his sacking as captain, but he was duly reinstated after a public outcry. Carling, like many players, was quite rightly appalled that the archaic leaders of the game were drawn from a particular tradition and that their adherence to amateurism was out of step with the demands made on modern players. In August 1995 the International Rugby Board held discussions with all national unions, and despite some opposition to the switch to professionalism, the decision was made to end the amateur only rule in rugby union.

The modern Olympic Games had been founded with a specific commitment to amateurism included in the rules of the organization. The amateur ethos of the IOC was rigorously enforced until the 1960s. In 1912, for example, the American pentathlon and heptathlon champion, Jim Thorpe, was stripped of his medals when it was revealed he had once played semi-professional baseball. In 1936, after his iconic victory at the Nazi Olympics, African-American sprinter Jesse Owens was stripped of his amateur status when he attempted to capitalize on his fame by taking part in paid races. One of the most vocal supporters of amateurism within the Olympics was the IOC President from 1952 until 1972, Avery Brundage. He argued in favour of amateurism throughout his presidency, and viewed professional sport as a branch of the entertainment industry. The problem for Brundage and the IOC was not simply the pressure from athletes who wanted a financial return for their labours, but also that the Eastern bloc nations of the Cold War period saw their athletes as warriors representing the values of the state. As a result the Eastern bloc nations were employing their athletes as civil servants or in the armed services specifically so that they could train and compete. In essence this policy made a mockery of the IOC's amateur rule. Brundage held firm to the end of his presidency, and in his final speech in 1972 he stated that, 'there are two kinds of competitors. Those free and independent individuals who are interested in sports for sport's sake, and those in sports for financial reasons. Olympic glory is for amateurs.' After the end of Brundage's term as President the IOC began making piecemeal changes to its amateurism rules so that professionals from a variety of sports could compete in the Games.

After the 1988 Games the rules relating to amateurism were completely abandoned. The ending of the amateurism rule however has been grasped as an opportunity by the IOC, and it has invited into the Games a number of high profile professional sports, such as the US basketball team, labelled the Dream Team, which was made up of the elite players of the professional NBA (National Basketball Association) and competed in 1992. In 1988 tennis was readmitted to the Games, and in 2016 golf and rugby will be summer Olympic sports. Critics argue that for a tennis player or golfer, whose year is spent travelling the world taking part in different tour events, the Olympics, rather than being the pinnacle of their career, simply becomes another ranking event. For the IOC the importance of such sports lies in their box office appeal. A game such as softball, part of the Olympic programme from 1996 to 2008, doesn't generate huge viewing figures, and thus revenue for the IOC, whereas the leading players of the professional tennis circuit battling it out are guaranteed to bring spectators and revenue.

What is evident today is that there are two sporting worlds. By far the largest, by number of participants, is the world of amateur, or mass participation sport. Here, millions of people play their games, for a variety of reasons, with no expectation or desire that they will be paid for taking part. The second world is that of elite sport. Here many athletes receive payment in the form of salaries from clubs, prize money, as grants from government or national sports organizations, or in the form of financial support for travel, housing, and so on. At the top, in terms of earning, is the professional basketball player or golfer, and at the lower end of the scale would be a national representative for a minor Olympic sport such as judo or shooting. Given that sport is now such a huge global business and that it is so present across the media of our daily lives, it would be easy to conclude that amateurism, outside of the world of the non-elite athlete, is dead. And yet the sense of an amateur ethos, with its attendant morals and ideals, has not only survived but prospered. In this, amateurism has little to do with whether money is changing hands, but instead speaks to the values that are imbued in sport. Those gentlemen who founded modern sporting codes and organizations were the custodians of the rule book, and they defined what sport meant. For those men in the modernizing Victorian era, and the administrators, sponsors, and marketers who have followed them, it is essential that sport portrays the image, even if in fact it is illusory, that it has a core set of values, principles, and meanings. This is why the IOC still speak to Olympic values, FIFA (Fédération Internationale de Football Association) wraps its games in the spirit of fair play, and the managers and owners of all sports, ably assisted by the media, cry foul when the moral codes of sport, which exist on and off the field of play, are broken. The 21st century athlete, who might earn millions of dollars in salary and endorsements, is still expected to support and represent the value system of the late 19th century amateur.

Chapter 4
International

With the emergence of national federations and associations to govern sport in the second half of the 19th century, it was perhaps inevitable that these organizations would look to challenge each other. The first recorded international sporting fixture took place in New York in 1844 at the St George's Cricket Club in Bloomingdale Park, and pitched a United States team against one from Canada. An estimated 10,000 spectators were in attendance, and some $120,000 of bets were placed. After three days of weather-interrupted play, Canada won. The match is important as it breaks the pattern, which was standard up to that time, of matches between specific local clubs. The organizers of the 1844 cricket match selected their teams to be representative of the nation with, for example, the US team being chosen from the best players from teams in New York, Washington, Boston, and Philadelphia. The game was also specifically advertised as a nation versus nation clash.

The practice of choosing teams to represent the nation was furthered in Britain. In December 1870 the captains of five Scottish rugby teams signed an advertisement in the sporting newspaper, *Bell's Weekly*, challenging any team selected from the whole of England. The challenge was taken up by an England side and the game played and won by Scotland in March 1871 in Edinburgh. As with the New York cricket game, the first rugby international was effectively unofficial as it had not been organized by a national association who managed the game. That situation changed in 1872, in soccer, when the English Football Association challenged a Scottish team to a match with the specific intention of 'furthering the interests of the Association in Scotland'. The game took place in November 1872, in Scotland, in front of 4,000 spectators and ended in a goalless draw.

As sporting clubs and associations spread across the globe, and in particular those countries of the British Empire, so international matches, in the form of touring teams making a series of challenges, began to emerge. In 1868 a touring cricket team made up of Australian aboriginals played 47 matches during a five-month tour of England, and in 1888–9 a touring rugby team comprising New Zealand Maoris played 74 matches in England, Ireland, and Wales. Neither of these tours were officially sanctioned, and both were seen by the organizers as financial undertakings where total gate receipts would deem whether the tour had been profitable and therefore a success. In both instances, given the public debate and fascination with Darwinian theories of evolution and the imagery of the non-white native, large crowds, some exceeding 20,000, would pay to watch the matches. The first formally recognized international matches that involved a British team playing one from outside the British Isles, which were sanctioned by and the team selected by a national association, took place in 1877 in cricket (Australia versus England), 1905 in rugby union (England versus New Zealand), and 1908 in soccer (on a tour of Central Europe, England played matches against Austria, Bohemia, and Hungary).

From the last decade of the 19th century sporting competition based around representative national teams or squads has become ever more important. Such nation versus nation contests served a number of purposes. At one level, the challenges issued by one national association or federation to another served simply to announce, in the early decades of sporting organization, that the national organizing body existed. From the earliest challenge matches it became clear that international fixtures drew a crowd, and became an important money spinner for the national governing body as spectators paid to enter the grounds. One nation beating another was culturally significant in terms of boosting national morale. Within a British imperial context the international fixture allowed the colonies, particularly in rugby and cricket, to upset the odds and take the landmark and nationalistic victory over the Mother country. Indeed, such was the dominance of the New Zealand All Blacks in their 1905–6 rugby tour of the British Isles, where they won every game they played (except for one game against the Welsh), that fears were raised about the physical fitness, indeed the apparent physical degeneracy, of the British male. Equally, in New Zealand the dominance and strength of the 1905–6 team, the measure of what it was to be a New Zealand rugby player, has become the foundation myth of that nation's identity.

Once sporting organizations, the media, and even politicians began to realize the value of international competition it spread from sport to sport quite readily. Groups of national federations came together and formed international federations that governed their particular sport, and arranged and sanctioned international competitions. Such organizations included the International Rugby Board (founded 1886), International Rowing Federation (1892), International Olympic Committee (1894), Fédération Internationale de Football Association (FIFA, 1904), Imperial Cricket Council (1909), International Lawn Tennis Federation (1912), and the International Association of Athletics Federations (1912). Such bodies, with their international reach, functioned as the regulators of their sports, making rules, adjudicating on disputes, and ensuring that their games were standardized wherever they were played.

International competition has become a bedrock of the sporting calendar, provides a focus for the community of each competing nation, and has also been understood as a way in which the nation becomes tangible. Eric Hobsbawm argued that the imagined community of the nation, which is made up of millions of disparate people, seemed more real (in terms of soccer) as a team of 11 named people. One of the appeals of international sport is that it does allow a representative team or player to symbolize the nation. As such the hopes of that nation ride on the success of the national representative, and victory, if it comes, can boost the sense of nationhood and well-being. Defeat can also affect the nation's sense of itself, and high profile underperformances, for example at the Olympic Games or at a World Cup, can undermine national confidence.

The Olympic Games

The modern Olympic Games, and their governing body, the International Olympic Committee (IOC), came into being in 1894 and were the brainchild of Pierre de Coubertin. A Frenchman with a passionate interest in education, de Coubertin had visited England. He toured several public schools while there, including Rugby School, where he was said to have been inspired by the reformist headmaster Thomas Arnold, and the way in which school sport was used to create moral and social strength. De Coubertin also placed great store in the sporting and philosophical approach of the Ancient Greeks, and through meetings with Dr William Penny Brookes, founder of the Much Wenlock Olympian Games in 1850, had been able to understand how a multi-sport competition might work. The various events and traditions that de Coubertin had observed came together in 1889 when he finally conceived the idea of reviving the Olympic Games. After a series of meetings involving figures interested in sport from across Europe, the IOC was formed in 1894, and, with the support of the Greek government, the first revived Olympic Games scheduled for Athens two years later.

De Coubertin and the IOC's thinking in these early years is instructive in understanding the spirit that is said to underlie the contemporary games, and also the ways in which the Olympics have deviated from their original goals. The Games, as conceived by de Coubertin, would have a philosophical underpinning, often referred to as Olympism, and much of his inspiration was drawn from his own romanticized reading of the ancient Games. He believed that the spirit of competition was central, but that the taking part was more important that the winning. He argued that the competition should be restricted to amateurs, and that the Games, building on the idea of the ancient Olympic truce, should bring about a spirit of peace between competing nations. Whatever the ethical underpinning of the Games, the first Olympics in Athens were deemed a success. Despite a relatively hasty process of organization, and a lukewarm response to the whole Olympic idea from some leading nations such as the US (which brought a team of only 14 that was mainly drawn from the athletic teams of Harvard and Yale), the Games were popular amongst Greeks and garnered a good deal of international press coverage.

In 1900 in Paris, and in 1904 at St Louis, the Games were side attractions to a World's Fair being held simultaneously in the host city, and failed to elicit any great enthusiasm. So disjointed were the Games in St Louis, and so subservient to the World's Fair, the sporting competitions stretched from the opening event on 1 July until the close on 23 November. Only 12 nations competed, and most with small teams. The US team, with 526 athletes, dominated the total field of 623 athletes. The 1908 Games were originally awarded to Rome, but were relocated to London after the Italians faced financial problems following the costs associated with clearing up the 1906 eruption of Mount Vesuvius. Although a host city of expediency, many argue that London managed to stage the first recognizably modern Olympics featuring 22 competing nations. It was also the first Games that featured athletes marching into the stadium during the opening ceremony behind their national flags, and as a result one of the first political disputes when the US flag bearer, Ralph Rose, failed to dip the

Stars and Stripes when his team passed the viewing platform where King Edward VII sat.

The Games were disrupted during the First World War, the 1916 Games originally scheduled for Berlin were cancelled, and the defeated War powers banned from competing in 1920 and 1924. In the inter-war years the Games grew steadily, with the Winter Olympics added in 1924, and staged at Chamonix in France. The 1936 Games were awarded to Berlin, and the ruling Nazi party transformed the Olympics from an international athletic competition into a mega-event infused with political rhetoric and spectacle provided specifically to enhance the status of the host city (and by proxy, the host nation). Conceiving the Games as an opportunity to showcase the positives of Nazi rule, the 1936 Olympics serve as a byword for a state propaganda display (Figure 7). Despite the intense politicization of the event by the Nazis, many of their innovations would become standard features of future Olympics Games. It was the first Games where there was a torch relay, the first to be televised, and, under the directorship of Leni Reifenstahl, the first to be filmed and produced as the documentary movie titled *Olympia*. They were also the first Games to be used as a political tool by other nations states with a point to make, and Spain, the Soviet Union, and Ireland all boycotted the event.

Given that the Berlin Olympics were staged to showcase the merits of Nazi ideology, it is perhaps the performance of Jesse Owens that best symbolizes the inherent contradictions of 1936. Given Nazi race policies, the party's newspapers suggested in the run-up to the Games that Jewish and black athletes be barred from entering. Faced with a potential US boycott, entry was left open to all, but the victory of African-American Owens, in the 100 m final, in front of Hitler, proved a visible rebuke to Nazi claims for the supremacy of the Aryan race. That said, the race politics of the US at the time were equally poisonous. Despite his propaganda boosting defeat of the Germans in front of the home

7. The Olympic torch being carried into the Olympic Stadium in Berlin, 1 August 1936. The Berlin Games was the first time there had been a torch relay at the Olympics, and through this and a host of other spectacles the whole event was used by the Nazis as a propaganda platform

Nazi crowd in Berlin, Owens was never invited to the White House by President Roosevelt, and on the occasion of a reception to mark his gold medal victory, after his homecoming, he was made to use the goods elevator rather than the one in the main lobby which was reserved for whites. While grandiose in its propaganda use by the Nazis, the 1936 Olympics proved that the Games were a political football, and that competing, winning, or even boycotting could score important political and cultural points.

Boycotts

The Olympic Games in the Cold War and Apartheid era were blighted by a series of boycott issues. In 1956 the Netherlands, Spanish, and Swiss all refused to take part in Melbourne in opposition to the Soviet repression of the Hungarian uprising. Despite these nations boycotting in support of Hungary, the Hungarians themselves did travel to Melbourne, and famously defeated the Soviets, 4–0, in a water polo game that became iconic for the sight of the Hungarian player, Ervin Zador, bleeding from a cut around his eye for the last two minutes of the game after being punched by the Soviet player, Valentin Prokopov. In Hungary the match is referred to as 'The blood bath of Melbourne' and held up as an iconic moment of resistance against Soviet rule.

The apartheid issue in South Africa was a central issue from the late 1950s, and in the face of boycott threats from other African nations the IOC had terminated South Africa's membership in 1962 (Figure 8). In 1972, and faced with another African boycott, the IOC also expelled Rhodesia from the Games, four days before the Munich Games began, as the other African nations did not accept the political legitimacy of Ian Smith's independent Rhodesian Republic. The South African issue reared its head in 1976 when the African nations objected to New Zealand's attendance at the Montreal Games given that its national rugby team had toured South Africa in the face of the sporting boycott of the apartheid state. The IOC argued that rugby was not an Olympic sport and had no grounds to act, but the African boycott went ahead and 20 African nations, supported by Iraq and Guyana, withdrew from competition in Montreal. The 1976 Games also witnessed the boycott of the Republic of China who refused to compete under the name Taiwan, a title change that the People's Republic of China had demanded from the Montreal organizers. The dispute only ended in 1984 when it was agreed that the nation would compete as Chinese Taipei.

The boycotts of the 1970s had been dominated by African issues, and while closely watched, had not directly involved the major Cold War ideological blocs. In the early 1980s the battle between the US and the Soviet Union over the latter's invasion of Afghanistan brought the two world powers into conflict and their

8. The 1971 tour of Australia by the South African rugby team was the focus of fierce protests against sporting engagement with the representatives of apartheid. The game in Sydney, in July 1971, provoked a wave of protests and many anti-apartheid campaigners were arrested

chosen battleground was the summer Olympics. Soviet tanks had rolled into Afghanistan in December 1979, and in response US President Jimmy Carter announced on 20 January 1980 that unless the Soviets withdrew within one month the US would boycott the summer Olympics scheduled for Moscow. Prior to the unlikely decision by the Soviets to cede to Carter's demands the 1980 winter Olympics were hosted by the US at Lake Placid. The Soviets sent a full team, including one of the most successful international ice hockey teams of all time. In the medal round of the ice hockey tournament a group of US College students faced the might of the Soviet team.

The game was played out in front of a packed, and patriotic US crowd, and became a microcosm of the Cold War struggle in which all the tensions surrounding the Soviet invasion of Afghanistan were unleashed. The US won the game and went on to eventually claim the Olympic gold. It was the US victory that was best remembered, and which *Sports Illustrated* magazine named the top sporting moment of the entire 20th century. After the morale boosting victory over the Soviets in Lake Placid, but an unchanging military strategy in Afghanistan, the US made the decision to boycott the Moscow summer Games, and embarked on a diplomatic offensive to convince its allies to do the same. The boxer, Muhammad Ali, was even dispatched to several African states to convince them to line up with the boycott. When the Games opened 65 nations had chosen to stay away, including close US Cold War allies such as Canada, Israel, Japan, South Korea, and West Germany. Nations that refused to fall in behind the US boycott chose instead to make gestures in Moscow that would demonstrate their opposition to the invasion of Afghanistan. The French, Italians, and others refused to take part in the opening ceremony.

In 1984, when Los Angeles was the host of the summer Games, the Soviet bloc responded in kind, and led its allies to a boycott of that year's Olympics. In total 14 nations boycotted due to what the

Soviet's deemed the 'chauvinistic and anti-Soviet hysteria' being whipped up by the US. While the 1980 and 1984 boycotts were direct products of Cold War politics, the political use of the Games by the US and the Soviet Union was part of a longer tradition of politicizing the Olympics, but also a indirect product of the events of 1972 and the IOC's response to them. The 1972 Olympics were hosted by the German city of Munich and were backed by the German government as a way of underlining the nation's postwar commitment to democracy and its optimism for the future. Horrifyingly, the Games were targeted by the Palestinian Black September organization. They entered the athletes' village on the night of 5 September and sought out the apartments of the Israeli team. Two Israelis who resisted the initial attack were killed instantly, and a further nine taken hostage. After a day of intense negotiating, in front of the world's media, it was agreed that the members of Black September and their hostages would be transferred from the village by helicopter to a military airport from where they were flown to an unnamed African nation. The German authorities planned to attack the helicopter after it had landed and free the hostages, but the operation went horribly wrong. In the event all the Israelis were killed, along with five of the hostage takers and a German police officer. For the Olympic movement the 1972 attack was the worst politically motivated attack made directly against the Games, and the first that had led to such killings. The German organizers of the Games, led by Willi Daume, President of the Organizing Committee, wanted to cancel the remainder of the Games. However, the IOC, led by Avery Brundage, successfully argued for a continuation. The day after the disastrous rescue attempt a memorial service was held in the Olympic Stadium and addressed by Brundage. He stated that 'the Games must go on and we must continue our efforts to keep them clean, pure and honest'. The Games were completed, although the Israelis and other teams withdrew.

The Brundage speech and the decision to continue with the 1972 Games after the killings were both applauded and condemned in equal measure. In retrospect it appears that the IOC had little choice. However, by continuing in the face of such atrocity, and having unwittingly given the Black September cause such a high profile in the global media, the IOC had proved to any interested party that the Olympics provided the ideal platform for the promotion of ideological messages. Although the political impulses behind the boycotts of 1980 and 1984 were entirely different from those of the 1972 attack, it was Munich that had proved beyond doubt that the Olympics were political, and that the delivery of any given ideological message through that platform would revive maximum attention.

Commercializing the Olympics

The fact that the Olympics had become such a globalized and media driven event by the 1970s and 1980s, although bringing politics to the fore, also served to transform the Games into their contemporary form: a mega-event underpinned by a media/sponsorship interface that creates huge profit and has made the IOC ever more powerful. Compared to the 241 athletes from 14 nations who competed at the 1896 Games, 10,500 athletes from 204 nations took part in the London 2012 Games. Such a growth in the scale of the Olympics has made it a highly desirable event to host, and one which can be used to regenerate the host city, create economic stimulus, and present a legacy to that city. Hosting London 2012 allowed for the regeneration of a large swathe of East London, led to the construction of a number of new sporting venues, provided social housing in the form of the athletes' village post-competition, and produced a profit of £30 million. For media outlets the Games result in some of their biggest audiences, and as such the cost of television rights has spiralled. In 2000, the US broadcaster NBC paid $705 million to screen 442 hours of the Sydney Olympics live. By 2012, and across all its television, digital, and online platforms the hours shown had increased to 5,500 but so has the cost. To cover the London Olympics NBC paid the IOC $1.2 billion.

The transformation in the finances of the Olympics came after the huge losses suffered by Montreal in 1976. It took the residents of Montreal until 2006 to pay off the CDN $2 billion losses that the games had made. The IOC made the decision shortly after those Games that they had to become more commercial, and began exploring how they could generate revenue from selling the sponsorship of the Games. The 1984 Games in Los Angeles were the transforming moment. The residents of that city, perhaps aware of what had happened in Montreal, voted not to fund the 1984 Games from the public purse, and so they became the first privately financed Games. To stage the Los Angeles Games cost $467 million, but from sponsorship deals, as well as ticket sales, the Games generated $1.1 billion in revenue. After all costs and outlays had been factored in LA84 resulted in a net profit for the organizers of $335 million. The IOC used the 1984 Games to launch The Olympic Partner (TOP) programme which runs its sponsorship, rights sales, and partnerships. The aim of the programme, which has been one of the most successful sporting rights and sponsorship partnerships in history, was to tie a group of core ten companies to the Games. In the first cycle of the TOP programme, 1985–8, the scheme generated $96 million. By 2001–4 this income had risen to $663 million, and in the 2013–16 cycle was worth $1 billion. All this has made the IOC a very wealthy organization. In the years 2009–12 it generated profits of $8 billion.

Such enormous wealth clearly makes the IOC a very powerful organization. With each bidding round to host a future summer or winter Olympics, vast sums of money are spent by host cities in trying to convince the 110 members of the International Olympic Committee that they are worthy of their votes. The IOC is often portrayed as an unaccountable body, which operates outside national or international financial and administrative regulations, that selects its own membership which is drawn from the ranks of the world's powerful, who in turn serve in self-interest rather than for a global good. Of the current membership of the IOC, which is dominated by Europeans, 41 members have competed at the Olympics as athletes, and many others are drawn from their national Olympic Committees or else served national and international sporting federations. Detractors argue that the IOC is in effect a small, elite private club, but one that holds enormous global and political power and is open to corruption as it is answerable to no one but itself.

Given that hosting the Games is considered such a prize, and is in the gift of such a small number of people, there have been regular claims that the IOC is corrupt. Investigations into the bidding process that awarded the 2002 Winter Olympics to Salt Lake City showed that a number of IOC members had taken bribes to secure their votes for Salt Lake. In response, six IOC members were expelled and a further four resigned. Similar claims have been made regarding the awarding of the winter Games to Turin in 2006 and the summer Games to London in 2012. Given evidence of corruption within the IOC and the scale of its financial interests, questions have arisen about how the movement is regulated, and how it continues to stand by its founding principles of Olympism. The Olympic Charter, which governs the spirit of the IOC and its Games, lists as its first aspiration that the movement serves to 'encourage and support promotion of ethics in sport as well as the education of youth through sport and to dedicate its efforts to ensuring that, in sport, the spirit of fair play prevails and violence is banned'. While this may be an entirely desirable and worthy goal, and one which the IOC does promote widely, it has to be asked how this sits with an organization that has been open to corruption and takes millions of dollars in sponsorship from global corporations that manufacture and sell hamburgers and soft drinks that don't speak to a healthy, sporting lifestyle, or sporting goods manufacturers who have been linked to exploitative sweat shop forms of manufacture. Also, given that the cities that bid to host and stage the Games take all the risks and incur all the costs of putting on an Olympics, why is it that the IOC solely controls all the sponsorship and media rights revenue?

FIFA and world soccer

In a similar way that the IOC has grown to be a global force, the same is true of the world governing body of soccer, namely FIFA, which has followed a similar trajectory and encountered many of the same problems. With the spread of international fixtures between representative national teams at the end of the 19th century it became clear that a body was required that would govern the game globally. FIFA was duly founded in Paris in May 1904. Initially the organization comprised France, Belgium, Denmark, the Netherlands, Spain, Sweden, and Switzerland, and was rejected by the British football associations. Prior to the First World War the global reach of the game was demonstrated by South Africa, Argentina, Chile, Canada, and the US also joining, and further growth was witnessed in the 1920s. In 1930 FIFA staged its first World Cup finals in Uruguay in which 17 nations from three continents competed. In the qualification rounds for the 2014 World Cup finals 207 teams drawn from all continents took part in the qualifying rounds . The spread of FIFA is such that Bhutan, Brunei, Guam, the Sudan, and Mauritania were the only countries that did not compete in qualification for 2014.

Soccer, in the form of national leagues and through the global governance of FIFA, is undisputedly the most popular sport in terms of viewers or players in the world. But as with the IOC, once FIFA began realizing the value of its product, so claims of corruption within the organization and its voting systems around the selection of host nations for the World Cup have grown. The 1966 and 1970 World Cup Finals in England and Mexico respectively were the first that could be considered global television events so far as existent technology allowed. In 1966 FIFA sold the European rights for the finals for $800,000. By 1990, the global television rights for the Italy World Cup finals were sold for $65 million and sponsorship of the tournament brought in an additional $40 million. For the Brazil 2014 finals FIFA were able to sell the global media rights for $800 million, and its three-tier sponsorship programme, an adaptation of the IOC's TOP programme (FIFA partners, World Cup sponsors, and national partners) is estimated to be worth $2 billion in the four years ending in 2014. FIFA is registered as a non-profit organization, and in 2012 its total annual revenue was $1.1 billion. With such large sums of money involved, and a number of nations lining up every four years to host the World Cup finals, corruption has become problematic.

FIFA has been accused of offering bribes and payments in relation to its collapsed marketing partner in the 1990s, International Sports Leisure, worth $100 million, and claims have been made that the bidding process that awarded the 2018 finals to Russia and the 2022 finals to Qatar was affected by votes being sold. Two FIFA members were accused of accepting $1.5 million to vote in favour of the Qatar bid, a claim which they denied. In 2011 the election for the presidency of FIFA was overshadowed by claims that one candidate, Mohammed Bin Hammam of Qatar, had offered money in return for votes. After an internal FIFA ethics investigation he was suspended from all soccer related activities. FIFA and the IOC, as well as other global sporting bodies, face significant challenges. While they promote their sports, and attempt to ensure that anyone in the world has access to their games, they also oversee a series of mega-events that are worth billions of dollars. These events interconnect national governments, with global capital and media, where it becomes almost inevitable that the fair play ethic sporting organizations wish to see on the field of play cannot be replicated in the corridors of power.

The move towards a full international programme of competition, which includes regular fixtures between nations, as well as qualifying tournaments that lead to a world cup finals every four years, as perfected in soccer by FIFA, is a model that has been followed by a number of sports. The focus on a competition that leads to the winning team being the world champions puts the media focus on any given sport, increases its profile, and allows the federation to maximize revenue from sponsorship and media deals. Outside soccer, world cups have been developed in a number of sports including basketball (inaugural tournament in 1950), rugby league (1954), volleyball (1965), alpine skiing (1966), hockey (1971), cricket (1975), and rugby union (1987). All such world cups spotlight national representative teams and, as with all competition, allow one country to claim the bragging rights. Alongside the world cup format, other international competitions are also staged such as the International Association of Athletics Federations World Championships, which have been staged since 1983. Here selected athletes represent their nation in the same way as at the Olympics.

In the world of golf, the competitive failure of Great Britain and Ireland in the biannual contest of the Ryder Cup against the US (begun in 1927) led to the revamping of the tournament so that a European select team has competed against the US since 1979. The switch has reinvigorated the Ryder Cup, made it highly competitive, and has seen its stock rise to such heights that it is now regularly referred to as the third most watched sporting event after the Olympics and the soccer World Cup. What is fascinating about the Ryder Cup is that the European Union team is made up of professional golfers from across the member states. For three days every two years these golfers representing Europe bring to life and represent a European identity that is rarely manifested in any other sporting or social context. In this golf has shifted one of its international tournaments beyond the national to embrace the continental.

While nationally based sporting competition will always have a place in the sporting calendar, international sport and the mega-events that it produces are often viewed as more significant. Such mega-events speak to sporting globalization and allow for the entwining of sport with the forces of global capitalism and politics (and the attendant accusations of bribery and corruption).

The audience may cheer when their national representative takes gold or scores the winning goal, but also has to pause and reflect on the meanings and values that link sporting endeavour with offshore sporting governing bodies and their close relationships with the inner corridors of political power and corporate wealth. The awarding of the 2014 Winter Olympic Games to Sochi in Russia produced a storm of protest over Vladimir Putin's denouncement of homosexuality. In a similar vein, the staging of the 2022 soccer World Cup in Qatar has been condemned on sporting grounds (the unfeasibility of playing matches during the scorching summer months there), because of the nation's human rights record and its appalling exploitation of immigrant workers (particularly from Nepal) drafted in to build the necessary infrastructure. Sporting bodies would argue that the awarding of major events to nations with questionable human rights records shines a light on the issues and produces the necessary reforms. This is a highly questionable strategy, and it appears that organizations such as the IOC and FIFA are motivated more by a healthy bottom line figure than concerns over their responsibilities. International sporting bodies are the first to preach about the positives accrued from hosting a major sporting event, yet it has to be incumbent on them to ensure that not only are stadia, infrastructure, and events delivered on time, but also that inclusivity and fairness, for all, are ensured in the laws of those states and cities they choose to do business with.

Chapter 5
Business

On 22 June 1938, at New York's Yankee Stadium, 70,000 spectators gathered to watch Joe Louis fight Max Schmeling, for the World Heavyweight boxing title. The fight was read by the media of the time as symbolizing the battle between American liberal democracy and German Nazism. That Louis was an African-American with restricted civil liberties, and Schmeling an honest and well-respected boxer who was manipulated in the name of Nazi propaganda, mattered little. Given that both boxers were cast as representatives of their respective nations and their political systems, there was an enormous thirst for the fight. The battle lasted only one round, with Louis battering Schmeling into submission after only two minutes and four seconds. The fight was one of the first to be broadcast live on radio across the European and American continents simultaneously. It was covered extensively in all branches of the print media, and brought in total gate receipts of $1,015,120, of which Louis won a purse valued at $132,000. While underpinned by the politics of the pre-Second World War era, the international nature of the contest, and the huge media interest that it aroused demonstrated that sport, no matter what complex identity politics might be attached to it, had become big global business. Such spectacles, whether in boxing or a number of other national and international sports, had been commercialized steadily since the later decades of the 19th century and, with the advent of television, would become ever bigger in business terms in the second half of the 20th century.

Commercialization

While the founders of many modern sports, organized for and played by gentlemen, believed that games should be amateur and have a core set of moral values attached, many others saw sport as a commercial opportunity. 18th century cricket and horse racing, in particular, took place so that prizes could be won, bets made, and spectators charged a fee to watch. There were also side opportunities for entrepreneurs who would provide players and spectators with food and drink. The activities of one man in the English Midlands, O. E. McGregor, have been highlighted as symbolic of the commercialization of sport from an early date. McGregor, the owner of the Molineux Arms and Gardens in Wolverhampton (now the site of Molineux, the home ground of Wolverhampton Wanderers soccer team) built a cycling track in the 1860s which became known as 'England's bicycle racing Mecca'. McGregor's enterprise was concerned with making a profit and his thinking was not shaped by the beliefs of the Victorian moralists who believed sport served a self-improving purpose. He had more in common with those who promoted other commercial leisure time activities such as the music hall or the theatre. In choosing cycling as the sport he would promote, McGregor also supported the wider development of the bicycle manufacturing industry. Sports goods, whether bicycles, bats, balls, or jerseys had all become industrially produced items during the later decades of the 19th century. In the same way that the growth of modern sport had relied on the forces of industrialization, urbanization, and the provision of leisure time, so the production of sporting goods was built on the same foundation: industry allowed for the cheap mass production of sporting goods, paid employment gave the consumer the necessary purchasing power, and leisure time allowed the players and teams to consume.

The sporting goods industry is one that has grown almost continuously in the 130 years since it first emerged. The golf equipment market is now worth $2.6 billion annually, the soccer boot business is estimated as having a yearly income of $19 billion, a major sports goods manufacturer such as Wilson (founded in 1913) has an annual post-tax revenue of $600 million, and in the US alone the total sales through sporting goods stores now amount to $42.6 billion each year (four times greater than the value of the breakfast cereals market in the US).

The sports business historically and presently speaks to two separate markets, namely the players (at whatever level) who consume goods and services such as equipment, specialist diets, sports medicine, and affiliation fees, and the spectators of elite sports who avail themselves of stadium tickets, media packages, sporting ephemera and memorabilia, and various forms of social media as a means of identifying with their sport or team.

Once sporting events began to be staged on a regular basis they attracted the support of people who wanted to watch. While earlier sports had been played on temporary grounds, the commercial impetus to profit from staging matches led to the enclosure of grounds. By building walls and fences around the field of play, the owners of clubs or the proprietors of grounds could then begin charging for entry. It was a rapid process and spread quickly across sports and nations. In soccer the first purpose built English ground was Everton's home stadium at Goodison Park (1892), Franklin Field, the home of the University of Pennsylvania, was built for College football (1895), the Melbourne Cricket Ground was constructed for cricket (1854) but was also the first stadium to host Australian Rules Football (1858), and in baseball the early US venues included the Polo Grounds, home to the New York Metropolitans (1880) and the first purpose built stadium, Forbes Field in Pittsburgh, home of the Pittsburgh Pirates (1909).

With the advent of a regular fixture list, so other commercial forces took advantage of sport. Around the world it was railway companies, above all others, that first saw the commercial benefits of being associated with sporting events. In Ireland, for example, the horse racing course at Cork had been opened in the 1865, and within a decade the Great Southern and Western Railway company had become a major sponsor of the races. In 1888 the company offered sponsorship of £200, which was a considerable amount, but their receipts for the day's passengers amounted to £700. It was the same across the industrializing world of the 19th century as railway companies, and within cities, tram companies, saw the profits that were to be made moving the crowds that wanted to watch sport (Figure 9).

9. Horse racing has a long history of operating as a commercial activity. A day at the races was a common experience for many across the globe where patrons could pay into the course, enjoy the day's racing, and, as here at the Santa Anita racetrack in California (1938), gamble on the outcome of the race

Other commercial ventures also supported and benefited from sport, including those in the catering trade. Pub landlords offered rooms for the use of sport teams so that they could change before and after matches, and the grateful teams named themselves after their hosts. In England some early rugby teams were named after the pub or the owner, for example in Swinton there were the Lions, in Broughton Mrs Boardman's Boys, and in Pontypridd The Butcher's Arms Boys. Brewers and publicans saw sport as a potentially profitable investment, and by the start of the First World War approximately 15 per cent of shareholders in soccer and rugby league clubs were from the drinks trade.

The close links that existed between the drink culture and sport would lead, particularly in the US, to moral reformers stressing the incompatibility of a night-time drinking culture with the supposed benefits of playing sport. But the provision of food and drink to the patrons of sport was essential to their business success. Until the 1980s the Football Association in England limited the annual divided that club directors could award themselves. The idea was to keep commercialism at bay by not allowing the club to become a money making entity. To bypass these regulations many club directors would award themselves the concessions contracts at their own grounds. The Mears family, for example, who owned Chelsea from 1905 until 1981, made their profits from their club by selling all the beer, pies, and Bovril at Stamford Bridge. In the modern era the stadium has been christened the tradium: a place where sport takes place but is in fact a business venue devoted to consumerism and the provision of services (hotels, bars, casinos, retail, conference venues, and so on) that may have little to do with the match day experience.

For many followers of sport, however, the pub or bar, in an age before television and radio, was important as it was where news about sport, particularly results, could be found. With the steady rise of literacy, and ever more efficient printing and distribution processes, various sporting newspapers emerged throughout the

19th century to capitalize on the interest in sport. Some of these were general in their coverage, while others were aimed at the follower of specific sports. Many of these newspapers, such as the Saturday evening results papers were sold widely, and often in pubs. The first sporting newspapers were those that covered racing and offered the day's race cards and results such as Britain's *Bell's Life and Sporting Chronicle* (from 1822) and *The Sporting Life* (from 1859). The sporting press was a global phenomenon in the later 19th century that spread widely to include, for example, Australia's *Bell's Life in Sydney and Sporting Reviewer* (from 1845), America's *New England Base Ballist* (from 1868) and *The New York Clipper* (from 1853), Italy's *La Gazetta dello Sport* (from 1896), and France's *Le Vélo* (from 1892). Alongside newspapers also emerged annual publications that served those with a passionate interest in specific games, and to many followers became the holy text for the sport. Particularly significant in the US was *Spalding's Baseball Guide* (from 1889) and in Britain *Wisden Cricketer's Almanac* (from 1864).

Albert Spalding offers an excellent example of how entrepreneurship and sport could sit close together. Spalding excelled as a baseball player, and was later manager of the Chicago White Stockings and a prime mover in the foundation of the National League. While still a player Spalding and his brother opened their first sporting goods store in Chicago in 1874. The chain grew rapidly and by the close of the 19th century there were 14 Spalding stores across the US. In 1877 Spalding began wearing a glove on his non-pitching hand, a glove which only his stores carried, and when he published the rules of baseball (1886) it was stipulated that the only officially sanctioned ball was one manufactured by Spalding. In 1889 Spalding took the leading players of the time on a world tour in an attempt to globalize the game, and to sell his products ever further afield. After the invention of basketball in 1891 by James Naismith, Spalding began manufacturing basketballs, and by 1894 the rules of that game also stipulated that only Spalding balls should be used.

When he died in 1915 Spalding had not only been one of the most significant forces in creating modern baseball as the national sport of the US, but he had, through his manufacture of a wide range of sporting goods and his dominance within the marketplace, amassed a fortune estimated at $600,000.

The close relationship between the press and the promotion of sport was perfectly encapsulated in France in 1903. A sporting newspaper, *L'Auto*, had been established in 1897 to compete with the best-selling sports daily of the time, *Le Vélo*, as part of a wider dispute over the Dreyfus affair. *L'Auto* (the anti-Dreyfus paper) struggled in the circulation war, and it was decided, in one last attempt to make inroads into its opponent's readership, to organize and sponsor a long distance cycling race around France. The inaugural Tour de France took place over 19 days in July 1903, and was covered exclusively by *L'Auto*. The first winner, Maurice Garin pocketed a prize of 12,000 francs, but the real winner was *L'Auto*. Circulation jumped to 65,000 and five years later had risen to 250,000. Most importantly for the paper's owners, their original target, *Le Vélo*, went out of business in 1904. The Tour de France grew to be the most iconic cycle race in the sporting calendar, and created an important sense of national unity, what Georges Vigarello called the image of France united by its earth.

The club

Usually lying beyond the gaze of the media, one of the most common features of the sporting landscape is the private club. Whereas a fraction of major cities may host a professional sports team, all of them will be the home to a network of clubs. Such clubs sprang to life in the late 19th century to cater largely for the urban and suburban professional classes who wished to play their sport in a convivial yet closed setting. Private clubs, catering for games such as golf, tennis, croquet, and so on, were designed to create socially exclusive enclaves. While sport may have been the *raison d'être* behind the club, it also served to create a space that excluded people on the grounds of class, race, gender, or neighbourhood income.

Private sports clubs, while serving the social niche of its membership, are also an important part of the sports economy, and dominate provision. In the US, for example, 72 per cent of golf clubs are private members' clubs, and while China currently is seeing a massive programme of golf course building it is all based on the delivery of private, member only clubs. Clubs charge membership fees, and these allowed them to purchase land and build facilities such as club houses. While some private clubs, such as the Augusta National (US Masters), Wimbledon (Open tennis), or Muirfield (Open golf), are iconic venues for professional sports tournaments, the overwhelming majority of clubs exist solely to serve their memberships. Clubs provide employment by way of green keeping staff, resident coaching professionals, and catering staffs. While the majority of private sports clubs operate on a not for profit basis, the club sector as a whole is vitally important to the sports industry. In New York, as an example of a major conurbation, there are 818 golf clubs. In 2007 the golf economy of New York was worth $2.7 billion and provided 56,000 jobs across the facility operation, golf supplies, golf course capital investment, hospitality, and real estate businesses. The wage income from golf related jobs totalled $1.6 billion, and the average revenue per private club per annum was $3.3 million.

The spirit of the 19th century private, single sport club was commodified rapidly in the late 20th century. Not only did private sports clubs emerge strongly in parts of Asia, Africa, and the Middle East, but new types of club, in particular the fitness gym, boomed across the globe. At the close of 2013 it was estimated that there are 153,000 private fitness gyms across the world with a membership of 131 million people and global revenue of $75 billion. The energy drinks industry, which is closely associated with the upward trend in sporting and gym based activity, was worth $37 billion in the same period. With the transformation of sporting and bodily practices in new markets such as India and China, which are turning away from their traditional forms of physical training, the fitness market will grow further.

The media

Despite the importance to the sporting economy of the private club and the leisure participant it is elite, professional sport that has driven the business. And no matter how important spectatorship was to the early development of sport it is the relationship between sport and the media that underpinned its growth into the multi-billion dollar business that it is. Initially in the form of newspaper coverage and later accompanied from the 1920s by radio, television from 1950s, and into the 21st century in the form of the internet and digital phone technology, sport and the media are inseparable. With each media development employed to promote sport, so the owners of sports teams have changed their business model to maximize profit. With the heightened, indeed saturation coverage of sport that the media affords, traditional revenue streams like gate receipts and media sales have grown. Indeed, there is a correlation in recent decades of the move of clubs to new, larger, purpose built stadia in line with the growth of revenue from media sources. These new stadia have in turn been used to boost revenue further through the provision of premium seating and corporate partnerships in the form of executive boxes. In 2006, for example, a standard seat at an NBA game cost $45, while a premium seat was $157 and a suite for the season cost $210,000. It is clear that television coverage and streaming, rather than keeping fans at home to watch the game, encourages them to spend high sums to access the 'real' thing.

Media coverage of sport has made the various games and players of each country the talking points of the day for the community. Radio and television exposure has made stars and heroes of the leading players, and in terms of the higher value of sponsorship that accompanies media exposure, it has made them rich. The media, once it realized that sport helped sales, has been central to the fortunes of sport.

Cricket, by the 1970s, was a firmly established television sport, and one that was governed by a cosy relationship between cricketing administrators and key state broadcasters. In Australia, Kerry Packer assumed control of Channel 9 in 1974, a channel that only had moderate ratings. Packer believed, quite correctly, that sport, above all else, would bring ratings success. In 1976 Packer lost out on the rights to show Australia's home international matches as the Australian Cricket Board decided to remain with the channel, ABC, that had always carried the games (even though Packer's bid for the rights was worth seven times more than ABC's). Irritated by vested interests in the game Packer set out to create an alternative, namely World Series Cricket (WSC). Packer offered contracts to the leading players of the day, far in excess of what they were being paid by their national bodies, and created a contest between teams of Australian, West Indies, and World XIs. He was opposed in the courts by the International Cricket Council, who also refused to allow WSC to use any grounds that fell under its jurisdiction, and many nations refused to select WSC contracted players for officially sanctioned international matches. Despite the opposition from the cricket authorities, WSC was a success on the field, packed stadia, and gained a big television audience. Packer also innovated, departing from the traditional whites that cricketers had always worn in favour of coloured strips for each team, and staged the first day–night matches under floodlights. In 1979 the Australian cricket authorities capitulated, readmitted all WSC contracted players, and granted Packer the rights to screen all official Australian international test matches. While the WSC experiment ended there, the process, which had been driven by Packer's desire to boost his viewer numbers, revolutionized cricket. Night games became a regular feature, and shorter games designed for television would come to dominate in the popular imagination over the traditional five-day test match. Television had transformed one of the most traditional forms of sport.

The 1970s also saw soccer in Britain in crisis. Crowds were declining, clubs were in financial difficulties, stadia were ageing badly and not fit for purpose and hooligans often garnered more headlines than anything that happened on the pitch. After a series of stadium disasters in the 1980s, and the ongoing violence associated with matches, many commentators began to suggest that professional soccer was finished and only decline and bankruptcy awaited the game. At the same time a revolution was taking place in television with the advent of the Rupert Murdoch owned channel, Sky television. This was not a terrestrial channel, but one of the first satellite channels to be sold to consumers commercially. Murdoch, like Packer in Australia, needed viewers to ensure he could sell satellite dishes, boxes, and subscriptions. Sport was his vehicle, and in 1992 the English Premier League (EPL) was formed by the elite English clubs specifically so that they could make a deal with Murdoch. The 1992 television rights for the EPL were worth £304 million for four years, a dramatic increase on the 1988 deal that the Football Association had struck with terrestrial stations which had been worth only £44 million.

For Murdoch and Sky the acquiring of the rights to the EPL was the making of a television revolution that was subsequently copied by his companies in Australia, China, the US, and elsewhere. For soccer it changed everything. Money flowed into the game, and revenues soared. New stadia were built, the best foreign talent was signed to English clubs, and the games were screened around the world, which allowed clubs to build their brand in new markets. In 2013 Sky agreed to pay the EPL £760 million for the season to cover 76 games live. Sky affiliates also screen EPL games live and in highlights packages to an additional 212 countries, reaching into 643 million homes and with an estimated audience reach of 4.7 billion people. For soccer the returns brought about by the relationship with Sky are obvious. The EPL clubs shared total revenue of £2.4 billion in 2010, and had the second highest game attendance (behind the German Bundesliga) with an occupancy rate of 92 per cent per game across the league.

Ownership

The revenues generated by professional sports teams, such as those of the EPL or NFL, are large, and in many cases growing. Sporting clubs and organizations, however, despite being run as efficient corporate entities (and not simply worrying about putting a team on the field of play), have different ownership patterns to many other businesses. Whereas most major industries and businesses float on the stock market and are therefore responsible to shareholders and answerable at annual general meetings, very few sporting clubs around the world are publicly listed companies on their national stock exchange. Manchester United and Juventus in European soccer and the Brisbane Broncos in Australian rugby League are among the tiny number of clubs that are traded stock companies. The remainder can be divided into two groups: those clubs owned by private individuals or consortiums and those that are owned by supporter groups.

With the attraction of professional sport as an investment opportunity in the late 19th and early 20th century, clubs were bought and sold in their entirety. Given the massive expansion of money in sport from media and sponsorship sources since the 1980s, recent decades have seen a fresh wave of club acquisition by individuals and groups of investors. In the EPL the majority of clubs are owned by individuals. Chelsea was purchased by the Russian Roman Abramovich in 2003 for £140 million, and he also covered debts of £80 million. In 2013 Chelsea was ranked the seventh most valuable soccer club in the world and estimated to be worth £588 million. Many commentators argued that Abramovich's success in buying Chelsea, winning trophies, and making profits led to an overspeculation in English football by overseas millionaires that has been injurious to some clubs. However, while some clubs were bought by investors seemingly as a plaything or an ostentatious sign of wealth, the pattern of purchasing clubs is now more regularly conforming to what could be understood as the US model. In the wake of Abramovich's success and the clear signs that there was serious money to be made in the sporting franchises of the EPL, consortiums have been purchasing clubs, as with the Fenway Sports Group's purchase of Liverpool (2010), the Abu Dhabi United group acquisition of Manchester City (2008), and the move by Randy Lerner, owner of the NFL's Cleveland Browns, to take over Aston Villa (2006).

The ownership of clubs in the US professional games of football, basketball, hockey, soccer, and NASCAR (National Association for Stock Car Auto Racing) is dominated by individuals and small groups, with the Green Bay Packers of the NFL a stand-out exception as it is owned by its fans in the form of small stakeholdings. Of the major franchises, 32 of them are owned by individuals who featured in the 2012 list of the 400 richest Americans including the owner of the Seattle Seahawks and the Portland Trail Blazers, Paul Allen (worth $15.8 billion), Robert Kraft, owner of the New England Patriots ($2.9 billion), and Rich de Vos owner of Orlando Magic ($6.8 billion). In the norms of US franchise ownership clubs can be bought and sold, but there is an oversight process by each of the major leagues. Such private ownership of major clubs around the world is an issue for supporters. The belief that the club is nothing without its supporters is one frequently expressed, but in effect supporters will have little say. If an owner wants to change the club's name, abandon long held traditions such as the colour of its jerseys, or move from one city to another, there is little that the supporters can do. Where this has changed is in the growing number of teams that have been purchased, often in the form of supporter's trusts, by their fans. Most of these teams operate in the lower leagues of European soccer, but where the model has succeeded is in

Australian Rules Football and rugby league. Here, clubs have long been cooperative ownership ventures owned by supporters. Importantly, given the need for financial stability in a relatively small national media market, Australian Rules Football and rugby league have also implemented player drafts and salary caps to try and create a level playing field where the financial advantage of the traditionally wealthiest clubs is neutralized.

The ownership patterns of professional sports teams, predominantly private, often cause consternation amongst supporters who worry, when a new owner arrives at their club, that they will not understand how special it is, respect its traditions, or achieve success. In this the supporters live in hope that their billionaire owner will be one of them, that is, a fan. The ideal owner is one who will have the deep pockets necessary to buy the best players, but who would also intuitively understand the club. That does happen, but for many owners, sports clubs provide status, profile, and profit and they are not involved in any club to subsidize its operations. In all this, and with sponsorship and media revenues, sport functions as a global business, albeit with some different rules and ideologies in place whereby success is not simply measured by the profitability of the balance sheet but in the winning of matches and tournaments.

Athletes and sponsors

Those who have benefited most from the money that is available in sport through salaries and sponsorship are the top athletes. Sponsors have long understood that linking athletes with their products can boost sales. In the early 20th century it was the makers of cigarettes that embraced sport by putting cards with pictures of the leading players of the day in their packets. Later came specific athlete endorsements of products from hair cream through to drinks and cars. Initially such sponsorship was frowned upon by the sporting bodies, and certainly advertising logos were not allowed on the field of play. This shifted from the 1970s when sport realized the value of its product and the television companies began offering ever more money and hours of exposure.

Players began to embody brands, first in the form of sporting equipment and then across a whole range of consumables. Companies such as Nike and Reebok built their brands around stars such as Michael Jordan, Magic Johnson, and Tiger Woods. In signing such global stars, as well as a stable of national athletes (in 2013, Reebok sponsored 12 major sports across the world, encompassing dozens of signature athletes and over 40 different countries), these companies ensure a high profile for themselves and their chosen athletes. In 2013, the golfer Rory McIlroy was signed up by Nike for $20 million per year, while other top earners included basket baller Derrick Rose ($260 million from Adidas), tennis player Maria Sharapova ($70 million from Nike), and the sprinter Usain Bolt ($32 million from Puma). In return for such riches athletes will play with the company's equipment (with logos placed on every conceivable part of the body), appear in advertisements, and generally endorse the values of the company.

While many athletes are sponsored by companies who produce athletic equipment, sports clubs, leagues, and national teams attract a different raft of sponsors. In the US, the NFL, NBA, and NHL (National Hockey League) receive the largest sponsorship from insurance companies, while in MLB the greatest revenues are received from beer companies. In all four sports the other leading sponsors will be from the fast food, telecommunications, and automotive industries. In other global sports markets the list will be little different, although in certain nations (where the law allows) gambling companies, drinks manufacturers, and tobacco companies will also be leaders (Figure 10). The latter two have been the cause of debate in recent decades with the question being asked, in various national settings, whether sport (an activity that promotes a healthy lifestyle) should be sponsored by alcoholic

10. **Like many businesses Red Bull has developed a close relationship with sport through sponsorship. In particular the company has backed a range of extreme and winter sports, including cliff diving, air racing, moto GP, and the Winter X Games. In its support of winter sports, it has brought a new audience to events such as freeskiing and given its best practitioners a high profile. Here, Bobby Brown is shown at the 2011 Snow Sports Training Camp at Squaw Valley**

drink or tobacco companies (products which are detrimental to health). In 2005 the European Union banned all tobacco sponsorship in sport, while France banned alcohol sponsorship in 1991.

The sports business functions, like most others in the world, in that the objective of clubs and franchises is, where possible, to make a profit. Yet sports teams are built to be put out on a field of play with the objective of winning. In this sport is different. Whereas in most businesses success is measured by putting opponents out of business or by taking them over, sports teams rely on the fact that they have an opponent. So, while Manchester United may not like Liverpool, the Red Sox hate the Yankees, and Carlton despise Collingwood, it serves the interest of no club to put the other out of business. Defeat them yes, bankrupt them no.

And despite the huge amount of money that is available in professional sport, only the minority of teams and franchises in many countries actually make a profit, with the remainder staying in business with financial lifelines from wealthy benefactors, supporters groups, or a long credit line from the bank. To avoid loss and indebtedness many leagues around the world have introduced salary caps and drafts which, in other businesses, would be seen as a restraint of trade. Sport is regularly cited as the third biggest business in the world, and while it manages its media and sponsorship deals, it will, in all likelihood, continue to grow in wealth. For sport has one advantage: while the movie industry can only produce so many sequels before the audience tires of the same format, the consumers of sport will tune in or turn up every week to watch the same teams, playing the same game, in the same places.

Chapter 6
Dark side

Sport is not simply about who wins or loses the game. While events on the field of play may constitute the limits of the actual physical sporting experience, the impact of sport is felt far wider. In 1950, for example, Brazil was the host nation, and hot favourite, for that year's soccer World Cup. They faced Uruguay in the final, in front of 200,000 supporters, packed into the Maracana stadium in Rio de Janeiro. The Uruguayans stunned the home crowd into silence, scoring the winner, with 11 minutes remaining, to win 2–1. In trying to explain the shock of the defeat for Brazilians, the writer Nelson Rodriguez noted, 'Every nation has its own irredeemable catastrophe, something like Hiroshima. Our catastrophe, our Hiroshima, was the defeat by Uruguay in 1950.' The comparison, while trying to capture the psychological effect on Brazilian pride, is ridiculous in terms of the human cost. That said, four spectators did die in the Maracana that day, three from heart attacks and one supporter who committed suicide in the face of the defeat. In moments such as these sport can profoundly affect people's lives and expose the frailties of the national consciousness.

As schoolchildren, spectators, through the media or as players, we are all exposed to sport every day. Given the ethical values that were enshrined in the origins of modern sport, the constant valorization of fair play and sportsmanship by contemporary sports organizations and the media, the games we play and watch are supposed to be 'good' things. However, sport has always had its dark side. Many of the ills apparent in society have historically manifested themselves in and around sport and, given the media focus, have been magnified.

The negatives associated with sport are by-products of the origins of modern sport. The legacy of the innovators of modern sport, from reforming headmasters, through to Corinthians Football Club or Pierre de Coubetin, is that they hardwired too many ethics (and rules) into the various games, all of which were underpinned by a contemporary snobbishness in attitudes towards class, gender, and sexuality. Ever since, any infraction of the moral code surrounding sport has invoked the ire of observers (and the custodians of sports), as the games are supposed to be pure in their sportsmanship. But they can't be.

The history of sport is littered with examples of athletes who have infringed the rules. In the golden age of English cricket, W. G. Grace, who publicly positioned himself as an amateur, was renowned for taking money on the side. His view was simple: he was the biggest box office draw of the day and his appearance would add thousands to the gate. As such, he should benefit. Gaylord Perry was a star baseball pitcher from the early 1960s and had a successful two-decade career. He was known for doctoring the ball and throwing a spitball, that is a ball covered in spit or grease. Constantly pulled up for the practice, Perry was ejected from a game for cheating in 1982 and his career ended shortly after. He has always been open in his admission that he doctored the baseball, but was still inducted into the Baseball Hall of Fame in 1991. Dora Ratjen, who was really Hermann, posed as a woman to compete in the Olympics (High Jump) in 1936, a ploy that, until the introduction of deterministic gender testing for athletes in 1950, was not unusual in its use. In 1986 the Argentinian soccer player, Diego Maradona used his hand to score a goal against England in the soccer World Cup finals (a goal he claimed was a 'little with the head of Maradona and a little with the hand of God'). At the Atlanta Olympics in 1996 the unfancied Irish swimmer, Michelle Smith, came from nowhere and won three golds and one bronze. Smith was later found guilty, in 1998, of tampering with a urine sample and banned from the sport. All of these athletes, and many more besides, were roundly criticized by those who frowned on cheating. The key issue with these examples, however, is that while in each case the rules were subsequently tightened, they all got away with their 'crimes' as, according to the interpretation of the rule book of the time, they'd done nothing wrong. Drug taking, gender twisting, match fixing, playing to the referee, all of these issues have plagued modern sport for a century and a half, and none of them have gone away no matter how the purists objected and the rule book adapted.

Gender

And it's not just on the field of play that sport has run into ethical problems. Sport was established by white men of a certain class so they could play alongside likeminded people. So what happened when the other classes wanted to play, or the colonized, the immigrant, the women, gays, or disabled? That has been one of the biggest historical changes in recent decades (or so it's claimed), and sport is now cast by its leaders as a world of open, equal, and free opportunity. But it's not. Women athletes are not paid equal prize money nor are they given equal access to prime time media (but then many observers argue that women's sports aren't as watchable). Take out the Olympics and Grand Slam tennis tournaments, where men and women compete at the same venue, and are therefore covered equally by television, and there remains not one women's sport which is given prime time scheduling.

However, on one night in 2013, on Australian television, a national men's soccer league live match pulled in barely half the viewers that the Legends (Lingerie) Football League live match in

Melbourne garnered. Clearly the spectacle of women playing football in their underwear has little to do with sport (and the Australian Sport Commission refused to add it to their list of recognized sports), and speaks more to entertainment and titillation. And yet sport has become a highly sexually charged arena. Fit bodies, ultimately a product of sport, are constantly marketed not as sporting, but as glamorous. The product has been labelled as spornography, that is, sports footage (or images of athletes) that is overtly sexual, containing scantily clad, attractive, frequently sweaty bodies. The results are evident in everything from David Beckham's adverts for underwear, calendars produced by English rugby and Australian Rules football teams, and the constant imagery of sporting women, in magazines and online, in glamour shoots. Danica Patrick, for example, a woman who broke into the ranks of the avowedly masculine world of NASCAR, is as well known for her modelling as her driving. Clearly the argument is made that this is part and parcel of a contemporary body obsessed culture, and that women athletes (and some men) can earn a far higher income if they market their looks as they can on the field of play.

Women were explicitly excluded from much modern sport at the time of its inception. Victorian men did not want women to play sport, and employed a raft of medical and cultural arguments to ensure their exclusion. Fear stemmed from concerns about the effect of sport on women's bodies, in particular questions surrounding reproduction, as well as moral qualms about the decency of having women's bodies on show and physically expressive and active. It was simple sexism, and despite the steady rise of women who did choose to play sport, and rule changes across a host of organizations that allowed them to (the Olympics first admitted women in 1900 on a very restricted basis, and in track and field in 1928), the bulk of women's sport has appeared a secondary concern in media and cultural terms. It has been shown that daily sports coverage in the US includes between only 2 and 6 per cent of content that focuses on women's sports.

In recent decades the fastest growing sports have been those for women (whether team or individual sports, or those associated with lifestyle choices such as fitness classes or aerobics), and yet the media (and the general sports/commerce complex) largely ignore them. This marginalizing of women's involvement (and achievement) in sport is part of a wider societal suppression of women's activities and success, which seeks to maintain the traditional gendered, hegemonic rejection of women. In all this heterosexual men are privileged and posited as the norm. Michael Messner argued that the primacy given by the media to male sports is closely tied to the maintenance of masculine power. This power is, in reality, a collective fiction, a narrow and archaic model of masculinity that appeals to men and boys. It is symbolic of cultural problems that mask, and then shore up, the uncertainties of masculine authority. Sport has been positioned as a contested terrain where gender is constructed in complex and contradictory ways.

As the numbers of women participating grows, questions have been asked as to whether this growth will be contained (as has been the historical experience), or whether it will lead to greater feminist social transformations. At the heart of this question is how far the quest for equality in sport is actually desirable. One school of thought argues that as women seek to advance in sport, in separate, women only sporting environments, so the men's sporting nexus remains intact and unchallenged. This in turn allows it to continue to replicate hegemonic masculinity along with all its associated problems. Sport offers a daily performance of public displays of a hegemonic masculinity, and given the division of sport into separate gendered spaces enforces a male power structure on and off the field. Eileen MacDonagh and Laura Pappano state that 'winning is male. power is male. Money is male. Physical dominance is male. And big-time Las Vegas-lined, media covered, sold out venue, sponsorship-rich sports are male.' They argue against this, looking instead for a future where sport is gender neutral, so that it does not function as a societal reinforcement to the idea that men are strong and women weak.

The constant use of the sporting environment as one which reproduces the idea that women cannot compete equally (a world view that is reinforced off the field) is deeply problematic. It is something that future sporting leaders have to address as the currently held dogma that divides men's and women's sport only serves to enshrine male dominance.

Sex and sexuality

The contemporary refrain from the organizers of sport, supported by a plethora of political and educational initiatives around the world, is that sport is open to all. It is marketed, in essence, as a democratic practice and a force of social positivity. Despite these core values that sport alleges to promote, there is a raft of evidence to the contrary. By the end of 2013 there was no active professional soccer player in Europe who was openly gay. Jason Collins, who had been the first gay athlete on the cover of *Sports Illustrated*, became a free agent shortly afterwards and was not subsequently signed by any NBA team until he was signed on a ten-day contract by the Brooklyn Nets in February 2014. Sporting culture demands team bonding, and this is fostered in training and in the atmosphere created around teams. Such bonding creates a 'strong dressing room', one where individuality is questioned and the goal is the creation of an aggressive sense of team. This is a hyper-masculine environment, and one that produces an environment that has no place for a normative sexuality but is synonymous with heterosexism and homophobia (Figure 11). This atmosphere is created by a culture, which is encouraged by trainers, managers, and owners, and has been heightened in recent decades as players have been granted star status, awarded huge monetary rewards, and surrounded by teams of agents, advisers, and lawyers. The upshot has been, most notably in professional and college sport, a dramatic increase in the number of sportsmen accused of gang rape, rape, and sexual assault. Team sports are conducive to a pack mentality. This translates off the field so that many sex scandals involving footballers include gang rape and the sharing of sexual conquests.

11. Justin Fashanu was the first black British soccer player to be transferred for £1 million when he moved from Norwich to Nottingham Forest. In 1990 he was the first professional soccer player in Britain to come out as a homosexual. He was widely criticized for the move at the time, and in 1998, after an accusation of assault, he committed suicide

The complexity in all this is that sporting stars are held up as heroes, a tradition that stretches back to the gentlemanly captain of the late 19th century, through to the first stars of the 1910s who featured on cigarette cards. To excel at sport, and to conduct one's self within the rules, was to be a role model. That tradition continues, and sporting stars are regularly held up, through education, in advertising and in the way that their life stories are told, as the perfect role models for youngsters. But what messages does someone like Tiger Woods send out? He was the first non-white player to dominate golf, win multiple tournaments, and, given his long-standing relationship with Nike, someone who had managed to make golf fashionable. Woods was a role model. In 2009 Woods's personal life unravelled and he was shown to be a serial adulterer. With all aspects of his life under scrutiny, even his on-course success was questioned, and accusations were levelled that he had used performance enhancing drugs.

Woods was not the first top sportsman to become embroiled in such a situation. However, Woods, through his close relationship with Nike, had functioned not only as sporting role model and hero, but was also the personification of a brand. Despite the fallout from his exploits, Woods maintained his standing, wealth, and sponsorship deals. The complexity with a case like Woods, and the aggressive criminal sexuality associated with male sports, is that without any action being taken against such men, including the loss of earnings, such behaviour is normalized. The role model is then not simply a sporting hero but a sexual predator. Young athletes learn so much of their behaviour from their coaches, from their mentors, and from the other men in their field. And yet the model passed on is often a negative one in terms of attitudes towards sex and sexuality.

Race

In the same way that sport has been used to reinforce ideals of masculinity, so it has been a location for battles over race. In the formative decades of modern sport many organizations and clubs barred different groups because of their race. Sport was constructed as a dominantly white, male pursuit. As a result golf clubs excluded Jewish members, the National Baseball Association would not countenance black players (from the 1890s until the late 1940s), and the Nazis, amongst others, pursed racial policies that excluded groups from all aspects of society including sport. Most of these exclusions have been challenged and formally ended. Jackie Robinson was the first black baseball player to join the NBA in 1947, Viv Anderson was the first black footballer to represent England in a full international in 1978, Chester Williams was the first black South African to play international rugby in 1993, and Roland Butcher was the first black England cricketer in 1980.

Despite these advances, and specific rules supported by most sporting organizations that reject racism, sport remains deeply conflicted in its approach to questions of race. In this, the type of institutional racism that blocked non-white athletes from competing has largely ended. However, the figures for the entry of non-whites into sport management remain very low. In 2013 there were seven African-American coaches in the NFL, three black managers in the 92-club English Football League, and no aboriginal coaches in the Australian Football League. The same is true of the various committees that run sports organizations around the world, with the number of non-white representatives minimal. Such under-representation speaks to the larger social problem that posits sport as a means of socio-economic advancement for non-whites, but that this advancement is not coupled with educational achievement. Also, as sport is a public activity played out in front of crowds, the racism present in society often manifests itself in the stands. In many countries, and notably in soccer, there have been regular and ongoing problems with non-white players being racially abused by supporters, and at times by fellow players. Publicly the soccer authorities take a dim view of such racism, but they have been criticized for not taking firm action against transgressions, preferring instead to position such racism as a societal problem and not one which it is their responsibility to tackle.

As with the gender question, it is all too easy for sports organizations to view the race question as something which is beyond their remit. Sport functions as a vehicle where the prowess of black athletes equates to success, but through the discriminatory practices in sport and the racism from the stands, sport also serves to reinforce crude racist stereotypes. Black bodies are viewed as sporting commodities (and this is valorized above educational achievement), and in the sport/commerce complex, racism functions in such a way as to maintain the racial status quo. As with gender, sport, rather than offering a platform for the genuine advancement of all, serves only to shore up wider negative stereotypes of race and the associated biological reductionism.

Cheating

A major ethical issue that challenges the meanings associated with sport has always been cheating. The rules of sport have always evolved so that what is meant by cheating is ever more tightly defined, and yet the attempts by athletes to gain an advantage over other competitors have evolved faster and in ever more sophisticated ways. Cheating has taken many forms across the decades, and one of the key battles in sport has been the crusade against the use of drugs and other chemical stimulants. In the early years of modern sport the use of opiates, alcohol, or strychnine was common and, at the time, within the rules. In the 1960s the use of drugs in sport, particularly amphetamines, became routine, with cases being recorded in soccer, athletics, and cycling amongst others, and the rule books duly redrafted. The use of anabolic steroids, popular amongst track and field athletes, especially driven by the need for success in the context of the Cold War and given the ever increasing monetary rewards available, became endemic in the 1970s and 1980s. One survey of Olympic athletes conducted in 1984 showed that 68 per cent admitted to taking the substance. The highest profile cases that highlighted the issue came in athletics and cycling. The 100 metre final at the 1988 Olympic Games was won by the Canadian, Ben Johnson. Within hours of his victory he failed a drug test and was disqualified. That the benchmark event at the Olympics had been so sullied caused public and media outrage, but Johnson was not alone. Of the eight athletes in that final, all but two would subsequently be found guilty of drug use.

Similarly in cycling, the question of doping, particularly in the Tour de France, has dominated discussion in recent years. Since 1998 only four winners of the Tour de France remain untainted by failed drug tests. Most famous of all was Lance Armstrong, seven-time winner of the Tour, who had always vigorously denied that he had taken drugs. In 2012 Armstrong was found guilty of drug use and banned from sport for life. The United States Anti-Doping Agency called Armstrong's drug use the 'most sophisticated, professionalised and successful doping campaign that sport has ever seen'. Armstrong's story began after the 1998 Tour was disgraced after a number of cyclists and their teams were arrested by French authorities for illegal drug possession. The victory in 1999 of Lance Armstrong at the Tour gave its organizers and sponsors the good news story it needed to counter claims that cycling was corrupted. Armstrong was enigmatic, and a survivor of a battle with cancer. He was the marketeer's dream and on the face of it, seemed clean. It is now clear that in their rush to renew the image of the Tour specifically, and cycling generally, the administering body of world cycling, other teams, and riders were complicit in keeping Armstrong's doping out of the news.

One man, the journalist David Walsh, wasn't convinced that a cyclist like Armstrong could come from nowhere, particularly after a battle against life threatening cancer, and go on to dominate the Tour in the way he did with his times becoming ever faster. Walsh spent years uncovering the Armstrong doping story, and the results were published in book form and serialized in the London *Sunday Times* in 2004. Walsh was castigated by the world of cycling, and Armstrong took the newspaper to court. The cyclist was vindicated by the court, declared a clean athlete, and awarded damages of $1.6 million. It would take another eight years before Armstrong was uncovered and before Walsh received an apology from the cyclist.

Armstrong demonstrated that the public imagination has a problem when it comes to our sporting heroes. Nothing in Armstrong's pre-cancer career suggested he would ever win the Tour once, let alone seven times. The sport, the media, and the public wanted to believe the story that a cancer survivor could triumph in an exceptional way, and the millions that poured into Armstrong's cancer charity spoke to the collective belief that he was a hero. And yet here was a man doing extraordinary things in a sport with a long history of doping. The very feat of cycling around France is an abnormal human activity, and many observers and ex-cyclists have stated that it is an almost impossible task without some form of stimulant. Despite all this, the public wanted to believe and were distressed when the dream was shattered by Armstrong's admission of guilt. Despite this, it will happen again, in some sport, and the hero will be shown to be a fake. But given the riches and the single-minded drive of elite athletes to win, we shouldn't be surprised that this keeps on happening. The spectator, the media, and sponsors all demand that the sporting star is an exceptional human being, the hero. But such exceptionality isn't normal.

One question that circulated around the time of Armstrong's unmasking was why would a cancer survivor further risk his health by doping? In fact, why would any person do something injurious to themselves to achieve sporting success? And yet they do on a daily basis. And it's not just the injection of drugs, but the actual playing of sport that is dangerous. As children we're taught that sport is good for our health, and yet in most countries the most popular sports are based around contact. A 2012 report for the European Union estimated that 7,000 people died each year while taking part in sporting activity. A further 6 million people across the EU required hospital treatment due to sporting injury, with 10 per cent being detained for longer than one day. The total cost to the budgets of EU nations of sports related injuries is estimated at €2.4 billion ($3.2 billion) per year.

Despite the cost of such injuries, the positive benefits to health from sporting activity is still greater. But what of the cost to the elite athlete? From school, through college, and in their professional careers, athletes in contact sports are constantly taking hits to the head and body. High profile deaths and injuries have been recorded in professional boxing, while in the US the NFL agreed, in 2013, to set aside a fund of $765 million to cover the cost of head injuries, concussions, and early onset neurological injuries suffered by 4,500 former players. In soccer, a game that has been heavily promoted as a non-contact sport in the US and hence popular with youngsters, the constant heading of the ball has been shown to cause brain injury. In Britain there is an ongoing campaign to compensate players who suffered neurological complications from heading heavy, old style leather balls prior to the 1970s. Recent research in the US has shown that 40 per cent of parents no longer want their child to play football at school for fear that it is too violent and will lead to potentially damaging concussions. On balance sport is clearly good for health, but potentially dangerous for the body, and one wonders, as health concerns mount, whether contact sports such as football will fall in popularity as happened with boxing in the 1990s.

Drug use in sport, whatever the health dangers, as with all forms of cheating, clearly flies in the face of the rules and ethos of sport. In essence sporting competition is supposed to be a level playing field where the most skilled will win out. By taking drugs athletes enhance their performance and win unfairly against other athletes who have played by the rules. Arguments have been made in favour of abandoning the pretence that there should be banned substances, and that doping should be allowed. It is suggested that such an approach would reintroduce a level playing field as all athletes could seek the same drug induced advantage. Such an approach is problematic in terms of the duty of care that sports organizations have to their athletes, as drug taking is injurious to health. But it is also a myth to say that open doping would be somehow fair. A heavily sponsored athlete from a first world country, with access to the best laboratories, would clearly take more effective drugs than an athlete from the developing world. In essence the competition would be one driven by access to the best pharmaceutical technology which, by the nature of national economies, would never be equal.

Technology

Such a technological gap is already evident. In sports that require expensive equipment and specialist training (e.g. yachting, cycling, alpine sports) it is the nations of the first world that compete and win. In the Paralympics for example, an event such as the 100 metre T44 category (for athletes with a single below knee amputation), athletes run on carbon fibre prosthetic blades. The technology is so good, and its use of energy so efficient, that South African Oscar Pistorious was able to make the switch in 2012 to the main Olympic Games. The blades dominate the Paralympics, but at a cost of $5,000, such athletic prosthetics are only available to athletes from wealthy countries. As a result the finalists in the 2012 T44 100 metre final were from the UK, the US, South Africa, Brazil, and China. Athletes with technologically weaker prosthetics have no chance, no matter how good their own physiology, of winning. The advent of new forms of technology and their management by sporting bodies is a constant challenge. In 2008, many of the swimming records at the Beijing Olympics fell as swimmers were using full bodied polyurethane and neoprene suits. These Speedo designed suits had changed the sport completely and, it was argued, because of their buoyancy, were allowing swimmers to race at 'unnatural' speeds. In 2010 the governing body of swimming, FINA (Fédération Internationale de Natation), banned such suits, but allowed the records of 2008 to stand. Formula 1 is a sport based on a competition between engine manufacturers and here technology is the key to victory. While Formula 1 functions as an aggressively global spectacle that has taken its procession of grand prix races to new markets in the Far and Middle East, it also adapts its rule book annually to try and ensure at least a semblance of a level playing field by attempting to rein in the most technological advances.

Whatever advantages athletes look for, whether through technology, diet, training, or cheating, the bizarre aspect of sport, perhaps what entrances so many followers, is that it is often decided by chance. One view championed in Michael Lewis's 2003 book, *Moneyball: The Art of Winning an Unfair Game* argued that baseball management to that time was flawed as it was based on the perceived wisdom of insiders who had an intuitive sense of the game. Lewis argued in favour of complete statistical analysis of player and team performances as the best way to understand how the game was played, and how his team, the Oakland A's, might best compete against wealthier opponents. The Moneyball technique has spread widely across many sports, and has noticeably begun to emerge in soccer. However, Chris Anderson and David Sally's 2013 book, *The Numbers Game: Why Everything You Know about Football is Wrong*, in accepting the value of data analysis, also acknowledged that 50 per cent of the game of soccer is down to chance, literally the luck of the bounce of the ball.

Sporting cultures

The sometimes random nature of sporting contests make them fascinating to watch, and while most leagues and competitions around the world are dominated by a small number of winning clubs, chance always offers the underdog the opportunity of victory. And perhaps that is why fans invest so much time and money in following unsuccessful clubs. They don't expect their team to end the season as victors, but they may savour a few days of success along the way. The statistics versus luck aspect of sport also talks to cultural difference. In the world of soccer, much beloved by most nations apart from the US where it ranks only as the fifth most popular sport, the game can be as much about the heroic draw or tie, as it is about losing or winning. There is something honourable, historically informed perhaps, in the spirit of a match well played, where honours are even. Such logic is at odds with all major US sports where every game, through the use of overtime or penalty shoot-outs, has to end with a winner or a loser. Statistically obsessed analysis and coverage of US sport is a fine art, where each performance is measured in minute detail, that seeks to negate the idea that a game might be won or lost by chance or fluke. A clear result should serve to reinforce the figures of the on-pitch performances and speaks to the winner takes all mentality that lies at the heart of the capitalist US society.

Violence

Such cultural differences have also been reflected in fan behaviour. While US sports followers may be quite vitriolic in their voiced opinions of players and their abilities, even to the point of hatred for their opponents, crowds at major US sports are not segregated, and incidences of violence quite unusual. Yet in the world of soccer, crowds are routinely segregated (something that is in the regulations of all national and international soccer associations), policing highly visible and violence a regular occurrence. What was known as the English disease in the 1970s and 1980s has now moved on to new terraces in southern Europe, South America, and North Africa. There are many sociological and historical explanations for spectator violence, with identity politics, socio-economic circumstance, education levels, and aggressive models of masculinity all being cited. Perhaps though there is a simpler explanation. Soccer, of itself is not a violent game, and its followers have often used the setting of matches to release their own aggressive desires. In US sport, whether in the brute force of tackling in the NFL, the regular player fights in the NHL, or in the crashes and explosions of NASCAR, spectators pay to consume performed acts of violence. Coaches, the media, and the fans encourage and, given the viewing figures for the NFL, expect to see and enjoy acts of aggression and violence.

The valorization of acts of aggression is problematic in sport. If the stars of today are encouraged to be aggressive, then what does that culture teach youngsters? Surely it tells boys to favour aggression and violence over respect. But a problem for elite sport is that the rewards are so high. Many sports, from boxing through to basketball, have been positioned as the way for young men (predominantly non-white) to improve their socio-economic standing. It's more pervasive than that though. Sport is also the way into college on a scholarship, it's the gateway to a short career where the rewards on offer are huge multiples of the average industrial world.

For parents it's a problem. Yes, encourage your child to play sport to be healthy, but at what point does the parent drive on the child to achieve that potential scholarship or sports career above all else that matters? At what point does the provision of support for the child, a healthy diet, and good equipment to achieve their goals, cross a line where the vitamin supplement is replaced by creatine or steroids, where the verbal encouragement by parents becomes abusive, and where the positive of simply taking part is replaced by the instruction to get stuck in and to hit them hard? For those athletes that make it to the professional ranks all such experiences and sacrifices would be deemed to be worthwhile. But what about the ones who don't make it, the ones seriously injured early on, or the African boys trafficked to trials with European soccer clubs who are abandoned in the streets of cities far from home when they fail to get signed?

For those that do make it and enjoy a professional career, a whole series of challenges await post-career, no matter how successful they have been. Once the routine of training and playing disappears, and the adulation and attention wanes, being an ex-athlete is a difficult struggle for most. Drink and drug use is common, and within two years of their careers ending nearly 70 per cent of NFL players have endured either divorce, bankruptcy, unemployment, or arrest. The figures in most sports, particularly team sports, are little different across the world. While there are strategies in place to assist athletes, sports organizations and teams have a greater duty of care to the youngster who doesn't make the grade and the ex-professional cut adrift at the end of their career.

Sport is often positioned as a positive force in society, particularly by those organizations that administer it and sponsors who bankroll it. Sport also mirrors wider social issues in society. In Europe in the 1970s and 1980s, for example, sport did not create the soccer hooliganism that would culminate in the deaths at the Heysel stadium (Figure 12). Rather soccer stadia became the venue for a generation of socially dislocated young men to engage in acts of both organized and spontaneous violence. In a similar vein sport reflects wider views in relation to issues such as race, gender, and sexuality. The question for the custodians of sport is whether addressing these wider societal issues are part of their governance remit, or whether they should simply restrict themselves to controlling their games and ensuring that cheating, in all its deviant forms, is prevented? Given the ways in which sporting bodies market and sell their games not simply as spectacles, but as fair and open competitions that promote positive values and attitudes, it seems inevitable that they will have to adapt far stronger approaches to genuinely deliver on the promise, the much promoted legacy, of what sport has to offer to society.

12. Soccer matches across Europe, particularly in Britain, were blighted by hooliganism during the 1970s and 1980s. Such violence reached its most awful zenith at the Heysel stadium in Brussels on 29 May 1985 when 39 Italian fans were killed at the European Cup final between Liverpool and Juventus

Conclusion

All of you have lost your way. You've become muddled.
Somehow you've forgotten what's important. I don't see a
room full of sporting legends here, I see a room full of
people looking for their next sponsorship deal, book deal, tv
series...You lot need to get back to basics, remember who
you are, what you are, what you stand for.

> Comedian James Corden addressing the elite
> of British sport at the 2010 BBC Sports
> Personality of the Year awards

Add more excitement to a match by watching it with
Mamee's popular instant noodles that come in six different
varieties...slurp up and cheer.

> Manchester United website explaining the club's
> partnership with its official noodle sponsor, 2014

The sight of a British comedian, albeit in the context of a sketch
at a major awards ceremony, demanding that the nation's leading
sports men and women remember what they stand for, was
telling. Corden positioned this elite as money obsessed and as a
collective who were pursuing personal riches over national pride,
who were more motivated by personal endorsements than they
were by acting as positive role models for the nation's youth. In all
this Corden was right. The public perception of athletes is that

they are a self-absorbed, money hungry elite who exist outside the bounds of normal societal behaviour. The sport-business complex has become such a parody of itself that perhaps even a comedian would not have dreamt up a joke involving the world's biggest soccer franchise, Manchester United, and its decision to sign up an 'official' noodle sponsor. The very idea that the excitement of watching a match could be enhanced by consuming a sponsor's product is absurd. But that's where modern elite sport is. An industry staffed by multi-millionaire players and franchises who take the money and sign the sponsorship contract, no matter what the product. Corden is right: sport has lost its way.

The 19th century idea of fair play and sportsmanship, and all that they entail, still shape the way in which sport is thought about. Yes, its followers want superb athletic performance, the hard won victory, and the demonstration of the aesthetic beauty of the body in motion. But they want all this competition, even though it is now firmly allied with the force of global capitalism, to be fair, to mean something, and to offer them life lessons. While the clock can't be turned back—there is no golden age to which they can return—they have to acknowledge what sport is. Yes, it has positive values that inform debates around health, sociability, and education. But at the core, much of the practice and business of sport is rotten, and does not conform to the ethical and moral ideals that it was founded on, that its organizers and the media promote, or that the public expect. Perhaps the lasting monument to the 19th century sporting male is that contemporary sport is still constructed as a vast and very public sphere that remains largely masculine.

Society accepts that elite sportsmen, from a young age, are paid millions for what they do. But people then cry foul when athletes don't live up to expectations, when they cheat, misuse drugs and alcohol, rape and abuse. But why should the followers and supporters of sport be surprised? Many sportsmen have low levels of educational attainment and emerge from difficult socio-economic circumstances, and are, most everywhere they turn, confirmed in a masculinity that is about dominance, entitlement, and power. Their life skill is their ability to run, jump, throw, or kick and they know their value is about winning over others. It's what they've done from a young age, what they have been trained to do and what they've excelled at. But at the same time society somehow expects them to have a finely attuned moral compass, to act as role models, and to live the ideal life. These are incompatible expectations.

A problem that lies at the very understanding of modern sport is that it was conceived for conditions and ideas that held sway in the second half of the 19th century. At that time it was men who embraced sport and gave it meaning, its rules, morals, and ethics. In the Victorian era, public spaces were powerfully constructed as male, while women were expected to enrich and decorate the private spaces in support of man in his public endeavours. Sport was very public, played out in front of spectators and a performance of male virtues: strength, courage, teamwork, and leadership. Sport was the public enactment of male leadership and brotherhood, one that encouraged a demonstration of physicality and strength, but that was supposedly controlled by an appeal to sportsmanship.

For women of the period, although things would slowly change, the domestic environment, being a good wife and mother, and knowing their place, was key. Women's bodies were controlled by medical notions of innate weakness and the centrality of reproduction to their being, and as such, sport was not considered seemly or good for them. Moreover, the idea of team sports played by women was inherently threatening to the hegemony of male authority. That anxiety still persists in sport today, where women's individual sports, which are seen as less threatening, are more highly valued than women's team sports. Sport excluded women from the start, and in doing so mirrored and perpetuated wider aspects of the gendering of public and private roles.

Whatever the advances of feminism in the last century or so, sporting women are still marginalized, their bodies, while athletic, are still sexualized, and the media, with a few exceptions, still holds that women at play, especially in teams, are not big box office.

It is because of its founding principles then that society has overblown expectations that sport will function as a wholly positive force in society. But strangely people don't expect the same sort of moral guidance from the stars of Hollywood or captains of industry that they expect from their athletes.

Sport, after all, is a physical activity still enjoyed as a natural expression of athleticism and energy, in many different forms and settings, by millions of people around the globe. As a mass participation activity it potentially provides a vital release from the pattern of the working week, sets important templates for healthy living for children, and encourages skill development and a sense of community. Sport allows the competitor, at whatever level, to appreciate the well-executed shot, set a personal best, or to catch the perfect wave. But this is sport as it is played on the ground and for the joy of it. As a business sport is entirely different. At the elite level, those professional sports that millions watch as spectators, sport is a multi-billion dollar global business. It moves the best talent from city to city and from country to country, and entertains its fans through a busy sporting calendar of league matches, tournaments, cup ties, and mega-events. It's entertainment on a commercial scale which, despite its supposed values and ethical codes, has few intrinsic values that are enforced.

Each of these elite occasions is accompanied by saturation level media coverage, an omnipresent level of sponsorship by major corporations and the urgent feeling, delivered to viewers, by the various commentators on television, in print and online, that this match or tournament that they are presently watching is the most important, most significant event, ever. But of course it isn't. Since its emergence in its modern form in the second half of the 19th century, and following its successful diffusion around the globe, sport has been a constant in shared global culture. It is inscribed with meaning and importance by commentators, but in reality each event is a passing moment. While the supporter's team may lose this match, there is always next week, next season, or next time. Throughout their lives followers accumulate an incredible memory bank of sporting moments, and in idle moments they may ponder whether David Beckham was a better soccer player than Bobby Moore, if Olga Korbut performed the perfect gymnastics routine, or Bjorn Borg was the most natural tennis player ever. This transience and need for immediate reinvestment and reparation is facilitated by 24-hour blanket sports coverage.

Through such mediums the personal narrative of sport that runs through the lives of many, mostly men, will have these memories added to, as sport is increasingly marketed as a site of endless, self-renewing possibility, providing a cognitive space to dream of improvement, success, and victory. There is a team or player out there, yet to be born, who will one day complete an undefeated season or play the perfect match. And on screen and online, 24 hours a day, the back room rumours and opinion, the wisdom of sporting insiders and pundits, bring sports gossip to life and delivers it with the serious title of 'news'. Public life is thus masculinized. Sport is evanescence in many people's lives, a temporary distraction from everything else that fills their days. For the millions of others who have no interest and care less, sport will inform nothing of their lives. But their mediation of the public sphere, via the media and the sports led business, will be structured by it anyway, as for instance, when weekend broadcasting schedules are dominated by men's sport, and when the hugely popular midweek soap opera is moved to accommodate the live match.

Where sport is most complex is in the cultural values, historically created, that societies have invested in it. While the active supporters and followers of athlete, team, or nation, want their 'boys' to win, they also demand that it is done in the right way. The expectation that sport is played in a spirit of sportsmanship is central to the rules, regulations, and ethos of all major sports. The administrators demand that rules are followed, the media will cry foul if they sense any indiscretion, and the public expects that the games they watch are clean and fair. However, changing notions of what is clean and fair can be read as an index of changing social values. For instance, discussions about fair and foul play can also be read as a means of mediating transforming social and political expectations. Sports related discussion now often focuses on how well an errant sports star (guilty of some off-field indiscretion or crime) has performed and how skilfully they (and their advisers) have managed to limit the damage to their 'brand' rather than the sincerity or appropriateness of their apology or amends.

In all this there is little difference in the motivation of players to fix games, nor the public/press reaction to betting scandals and match fixing (or any other infraction of the rules) across time or place. After all, the players of Chicago Black Sox took money to throw the 1919 World Series for the same reasons that Pakistani cricketers bowled a series of no balls in 2010: they were being paid by gamblers. Equally the reaction was similar in both cases, with official investigations, political questioning, and police involvement all responding to the howls of public and media contempt for athletes who were more interested in financial reward than the integrity of the game. The sporting public does not like cheats who destroy the integrity of the game. Taking advantage of a referee's bad call, or feigning injury to kill time, is one thing: it's called competitive advantage. Undermining what is supposed to be a fair contest, to subvert the result solely for your own financial gain, is repugnant. In the context of the Chicago Black Sox scandal it was best summed up by the widely disseminated, but apocryphal story, of a young boy questioning the Sox's outfielder, Joe Jackson, about the charge that the Sox had thrown the game: 'Say it ain't so, Joe.' It matters not whether the exchange ever happened. But rather that the scene perfectly encapsulated the dreams and hopes that a child (and indeed many adults) held as representing their understanding of the inherent decency of sport, and its stars, which could all be so cruelly destroyed by a self-serving professional who wanted a better payday than the one that winning fairly might have offered.

And yet, despite all this corruption, sport is a competition which stands to bring glory, social standing, and financial reward to its, largely male, able-bodied, participants. Each athlete and team searches for competitive advantage: extra training, a better diet, employing the best trainer, committing a foul out of sight of the referee, using the best available technology, taking drugs, or cheating. Sport still demands that modern athletes conduct themselves like the ideal Victorian amateur gentlemen, but given that winning is the goal, this is an unlikely scenario. But sport, despite all its rules, is not an equal competition. Socio-economic wealth, education levels, access, facilities, race, sexuality, gender, physical ability, mental or physical disability: all these factors, and many more, will determine how well any given individual will be able to access sport and whether they will succeed. Sport, whatever the score, and no matter who wins, is not, and never can be, a level playing field.

Further reading

General

Eric Anderson, *In the Game: Gay Athletes and the Cult of Masculinity* (New York, 2005).

William J. Baker, *Sports in the Western World* (Chicago, 1988).

Amy Bass (ed.), *In the Game: Race, Identity and Sports in the Twentieth Century* (New York, 2005).

Douglas Booth, *The Field: Truth and Fiction in Sports History* (London, 2005).

Susan Cahn, *Coming on Strong: Gender and Sexuality in Twentieth Century Women's Sport* (Cambridge, 1995).

Jay Coakley and Eric Dunning (eds.), *Handbook of Sports Studies* (London, 2000).

Tony Collins, *Sport in Capitalist Society* (London, 2013).

David Goldblatt, *The Ball is Round: A Global History of Football* (London, 2007).

Hans Ulrich Gumbrecht, *In Praise of Athletic Beauty* (Cambridge, 2006).

Allen Guttmann, *Sports: The First Five Millennia* (Amherst, 2005).

Richard Holt, *Sport and the British* (Oxford, 1981).

Jukes Tygiel, *Past Times: Baseball as History* (New York, 2001).

Origins of sport

Emma Griffin, *England's Revelry: A History of Popular Sports and Pastimes, 1660–1830* (Oxford, 2005).

Allen Guttmann, *From Ritual to Record: The Nature of Modern Sports* (New York, 1978).

David Potter and D. J. Mattingly (eds.), *Life, Death and Entertainment in the Roman Empire* (Ann Arbor, 1999).

Nigel Spivey, *The Ancient Olympics* (Oxford, 2004).

Modern sport

Robert Malcolmson, *Popular Recreations in English Society 1700–1850* (Cambridge, 1973).

Michael Mandelbaum, *The Meaning of Sports: Why Americans Watch Baseball, Football and Basketball and What They See When They Do* (New York, 2004).

Benjamin Rader, *American Sports: From the Age of Folk Games to the Age of Televised Sports* (New York, 2003).

Neil Tranter, *Sport, Economy and Society in Britain, 1750–1914* (Cambridge, 1998).

Amateurs and professionals

Lincoln Allison, *Amateurism: An Analysis and a Defence* (London, 2000).

James Huntington-Whiteley and Richard Holt, *The Book of British Sporting Heroes* (London, 1998).

S. W. Pope, *Patriotic Games: Sporting Traditions in the American Imagination, 1876–1926* (New York, 1997).

Dilwyn Porter and Adrian Smith (eds.), *Amateurs and Professionals in Post-War British Sport* (London, 2000).

Steven A. Reiss, *Sport in Industrial America, 1850–1920* (New York, 2013).

International sport

Jean-Loup Chappelet, *The International Olympic Committee and the Olympic System: The Governance of World Sport* (London, 2008).

Maurice Roche, *Mega-Events and Modernity: Olympics and Expos in the Growth of Global Culture* (London, 2002).

John Sugden and Alan Tomlinson, *FIFA and the Contest for World Football: Who Rules the People's Game?* (London, 1998).

Alan Tomlinson and Christopher Young (eds.), *National Identity and Global Sporting Events: Culture, Politics and Spectacle in the Olympics and the Football World Cup* (New York, 2006).

The sport business

David Carter, *Money Games: Profiting from the Convergence of Sports and Entertainment* (Stanford, 2010).

Simon Kuper and Stefan Szymanski, *Soccernomics: Why England Loses, Why Germany and Brazil Win, and Why the US, Japan, Australia, Turkey—and Even Iraq—Are Destined to Become the Kings of World's Most Popular Sport* (London, 2009).

Gary Whannel, *Fields in Vision: Television, Sport and Cultural Transformation* (London, 2013).

Sport and society

Ellen McDonagh and Laura Pappano, *Playing with the Boys: Why Separate Is Not Equal in Sports* (New York, 2008).

Michael A. Messner, *Out of Play: Critical Essays on Gender and Sport* (New York, 2007).

Roberta Park and Patricia Vertinsky (eds.), *Women, Sport, Society: Further Reflections, Reaffirming Mary Wollstonecraft* (London, 2013).

Richard Pound, *Inside Dope: How Drugs Are the Biggest Threat to Sports, Why You Should Care and What Can Be Done about Them* (New York, 2010).

Mike Rowbottom, *Foul Play: The Dark Arts of Cheating in Sport* (London, 2013).

Index

Sport

Woods, Tiger 3, 95, 105
wrestling 9, 10, 12

Y

Yale University 33, 67

YMCA 44
yoga 7

Z

Zador, Ervin 69

SOCIAL MEDIA
Very Short Introduction

Join our community

www.oup.com/vsi

- Join us online at the official Very Short Introductions **Facebook** page.
- Access the thoughts and musings of our authors with our online **blog**.
- Sign up for our monthly **e-newsletter** to receive information on all new titles publishing that month.
- Browse the full range of Very Short Introductions online.
- Read **extracts** from the Introductions for free.
- Visit our library of **Reading Guides**. These guides, written by our expert authors will help you to question again, why you think what you think.
- If you are a teacher or lecturer you can order inspection copies quickly and simply via our website.